THE WHISPERING GALLERY

Hesketh Pearson was born in 1887, and after attending the Bedford Grammar School he took his first job in a shipping office. In 1911 Pearson turned to the theatre, but his acting career was interrupted by the First World War; he joined the army and fought in Mesopotamia and Persia from 1914 to 1918. Pearson then returned to the stage as both an actor and a director. It was not until 1921 that he began his career as a writer, with *Modern Men and Mummers* (1921), a gallery of amusing portraits of his prominent contempories in the theatre. Thereafter Pearson's output largely consisted of lively and popular biographies of famous literary and artistic figures. He died in 1964, and his autobiography, *Hesketh Pearson by Himself*, appeared a year later.

ALSO BY HESKETH PEARSON

Doctor Darwin (1930)
Gilbert and Sullivan (1935)
A Life of Shakespeare (1942)
G.B.S.: A Full-Length Portrait (1942)
Conan Doyle: His Life and Art (1943)
The Life of Oscar Wilde (1946)
The Man Whistler (1952)
Henry of Navarre (1963)
Hesketh Pearson by Himself (1965)

Michael Holroyd was born in 1935 in London. He is best known for his biographies of three outstanding literary and artistic figures, Augustus John, Bernard Shaw and Lytton Strachey, and an autobiography *Basil Street Blues*.

THE WHISPERING GALLERY

Being Leaves from a Diplomat's Diary

---

by

Hesketh Pearson

Introduced by

Michael Holroyd

**PHOENIX
PRESS**

5 UPPER SAINT MARTIN'S LANE
LONDON
WC2H 9EA

A PHOENIX PRESS PAPERBACK

First published in Great Britain
by John Lane, The Bodley Head Ltd in 1926
This paperback edition published in 2000
by Phoenix Press,
a division of The Orion Publishing Group Ltd,
Orion House, 5 Upper St Martin's Lane,
London WC2H 9EA

A CIP catalogue record for this book
is available from the British Library.

Printed and bound in Great Britain by
Butler & Tanner Ltd, Frome and London

ISBN 1 84212 197 9

CONTENTS

CONTENTS

INTRODUCTION

The Whispering Gallery is a curiosity. It purports to be some frank, often indiscreet, occasionally sensational pages from the diary of a highly-distinguished, retired diplomat who, at the time of the book's brief publication at the end of 1926, was apparently determined to conceal his identity behind an anonymous title page. 'My life has been almost wholly passed in the midst of big events and among the leading actors, the controlling agents, of those events,' he writes with a pleasing *double entendre* that went unrecognised by early readers of the book. For *The Whispering Gallery* was actually an audacious, satirical work of make believe, composed by Hesketh Pearson, an actor then in his late thirties, who had indeed passed most of his career among leading actors in the midst of big events on stage, and also with the 'controlling agents' of those events, the playwrights. Pearson was eventually to become better known as a biographer than an actor, being poised in the late 1920s between these two careers. But *The Whispering Gallery* could hardly have been a more ill-starred curtain raiser to his writing life. Why then had he done it? The answer appears to form part of a pattern in his life. For this was not the first time he had risked his reputation and courted bankruptcy.

He had been born in 1887 at Hawford, near Worcester, one of the four children of a gentleman farmer, churchwarden and keen amateur sportsman, and his second wife, the daughter of a clergyman.

In his autobiography, Pearson describes his father, nicknamed 'Pompous Pearson', as being 'invariably friendly but rather remote and awe-inspiring', while his mother who, he suspected, never wanted children, he calls 'wonderfully forbearing' – adding quickly that he 'never lacked her love'. But though his childhood at home was not unhappy, he increasingly felt a need to distance himself from this 'rather matter-of-fact and undemonstrative' family. He never shared his father's solemn passion for sport, while 'religion made no impression on me whatever'. In his biographies he tended to belittle the influence of parents on children, preferring to believe that 'one inherits more from a few million ancestors than from two people immediately responsible for one's birth'.

The unhappiest years of Hesketh Pearson's life were undoubtedly those he spent at school. He went first to Orkney House School, a 'place of torment' run by a sadistic headmaster devoted to the flogging of young boys. But however ferociously he was punished, 'I simply could not keep out of mischief'. He seemed fated to do everything of which adults disapproved. He was incurably adventurous and almost unteachable, blessed with a happy nature, yet vulnerable to violent spasms of temper, suddenly-aroused and quickly-forgotten, that would recur over most of his adult life. 'I cannot explain the cause of my tempers,' he wrote in his autobiography, *Hesketh Pearson by Himself*, though he thought they might have been 'exacerbated by my hatred of compulsion, and school was one long compulsion. I was a born rebel, and I rebelled against a discipline that seemed to me futile.'

After five years at Orkney House School, he went to Bedford Grammar School where, though he learnt little, he was happier. He had initially been placed in the Civil and Military section of the school from where it was hoped he would go on to Sandhurst, but when this plan collapsed, and after his father had failed to persuade him to read the classics with a view to becoming a clergyman, he was transferred to the Mercantile Class where he languished amiably enough. Much of the literature he was taught, from Shakespeare to Scott, which he later came to love, he loathed at school because of the impersonal way it was presented. Instead, he found his own authors, beginning with the detective stories and historical romances of Conan Doyle and Stanley Weyman, then Victor Hugo's *Les Misérables*, and the novels of Dumas and Balzac which he read in French, having picked up the language not at school but during some holidays in France.

Pearson emerged from his formal education as a man without qualifications. He drifted into a city shipping office from which, after two and a half years, at the age of twenty-one, he was liberated by a legacy of a thousand pounds from an aunt. This he spent travelling in South America, the United States and Canada, returning in 1908 to manage a car showroom in Brighton belonging to one of his brothers. By 1910, having helped this business into liquidation, he was penniless and obliged to live again with his parents.

But these had not been wasted years. He had enjoyed several happy educative affaires, and also provided himself with an artistic education by reading widely, listening to music, and becoming increasingly responsive to the English landscape. He was particularly influenced by the work of Oscar Wilde and Bernard Shaw, and the Shakespearian productions of Beerbohm Tree. Wilde, Shakespeare, Tree and Shaw, all of them to be subjects of his biographies were the four authors of what he called his 'revelations', leading him to maturity.

In 1911, regardless of his father's opposition and despite his own lack of training, Pearson joined Beerbohm Tree's theatre company at His Majesty's, later acting in Harley Granville Barker's productions at St James's and also working with Sir George Alexander whom he often understudied. In one of his first speaking parts, a minor character in Alfred Sutro's *The Builder of Bridges*, he met and fell in love with a tall, dark actress, Gladys Gardner, with whom, as 'a prudent preliminary' to marriage, he had an affaire. The play was touring the country, and late one night, sitting on the sands at Scarborough, he asked her to marry him. She accepted, which was just as well because as a result of Pearson's prudence she was already pregnant. They were married in the summer of 1912 and their son Henry was born 'prematurely' seven months later.

His stage career was halted by the war, but in 1915 he was invalided out of the infantry suffering from tuberculosis. The army, he felt, re-imposed many of the senseless disciplines of school, and he proved to be a mutinous soldier. Nevertheless, he volunteered the following year for the Army Service Corps. For three years he served in Mesopotamia and Persia, rising from private soldier to captain, being cited for 'gallant and distinguished service in the field' and awarded the Military Cross (something he omitted to enter in *Who's Who* and did not allude to in his autobiography). What he did describe was his near-death from a combination of dysentery, malaria, septic sores and a serious head wound. He attributed his miraculous recovery to reciting (even under the anaesthetic) the plays of Shakespeare, several of which he knew by heart.

After the war he returned to the stage. But though he was slowly gaining a fair reputation as an actor, it was erratic work and he found difficulty making enough regular income for his family. Fortunately he was also writing. During the war, as his biographer Ian Hunter writes, 'he had been sending dispatches and feature articles back to the *Star* and the *Manchester Guardian* ... on topics as varied as Egyptian archaeology and an Oriental version of *Hamlet* performed in Baghdad'. Afterwards he went on to publish two books arising from his wartime experiences.

A Persian Critic, is a series of colloquies, some of which had previously appeared in *The Times*, between a host and guest and which, we are asked to believe, take place after the author, caught stealing mulberries from a garden in Hermanshah, is invited by the owner of the tree into his house to discourse on English and French literature.

The second book, *Iron Rations*, which Pearson dedicated to his batman, is a mixture of fiction and non-fiction, a dozen short stories followed by nine essays, which he wanted to preface with a variation of the customary disclaimer: 'When I say that the characters and episodes in this book are imaginary and have no relation whatsoever to real people and actual happenings, it will of course be understood that both characters and episodes are straight from life and are strictly true in every detail.' The publisher, however, objected, and readers of the book are simply warned that 'the characters are imaginary' and that the author 'has selected their names at random'.

Both books, which were politely and even favourably reviewed, had been preceded in 1921 by a far more controversial volume. *Modern Men and Mummers*, which largely derived from Pearson's pre-war years on the stage, may be regarded as a forerunner to *The Whispering Gallery*. On the front jacket, the publishers Allen and Unwin declared that though most of the subjects of his essays were used to the limelight, the author 'throws it where it is least expected, turns it on humorously, maliciously, with Puck-like ingenuity ...'. The tone varies between the fulsomely eulogistic (on Frank Harris and Bernard Shaw who 'corrected' the essay on himself as he would later 'correct' Pearson's famous biography of him) to the impertinent and opinionated. There is an amusing interview with Lytton Strachey whose influence on Pearson, together with that of Frank Harris, is partly responsible for both *Modern Men and Mummers* and *The Whispering Gallery*. These writers, Pearson believed, had liberated non-fiction from the obsequious routine of hagiography and transformed biography itself into an art that could be as imaginative and free as the novel.

The best essays in *Modern Men and Mummers* are those about the actor-managers and playwright-producers whom Pearson had had an opportunity to observe closely. Though they are on the whole affectionate, they also contain passages of criticism the harshness of which was then unusual. Even his hero Beerbohm Tree is described as a 'big baby' whose whimsicality was 'unbearable' during the rehearsals of tragedies, and who had been responsible for many 'atrociously bad plays'. George Alexander is depicted as an artistically immature snob who traded in 'the drama of the genteel', catering to London Society in its theatre-going 'as the manager of the Savoy Hotel catered to the taste and foibles of that Society in its restaurant-going'. We are also shown the popular actor-manager Frank

Benson, who had been responsible for spreading Shakespeare through the country and training many fine Shakespearian actors, as being impossible to understand on stage, not so much because he bellowed incoherently but because he misquoted every other line – and he always took the chief parts.

Pearson seems to have been indifferent to public opinion and, as he later admitted, 'was lucky to keep out of the law courts'. There was, as one reviewer wrote admiringly, a libel on every page. After publication he did receive a threat of legal proceedings from the financier and politician Horatio Bottomley which would almost certainly have landed him in court if Bottomley himself hadn't shortly afterwards landed in prison. By an odd stroke of irony, the book led to an offer from the magazine *John Bull*, which Bottomley had founded in 1906, for Pearson to write pen portraits of famous people each week for the next three years.

The famous people, or 'Modern Men' in *Modern Men and Mummers*, had attracted Pearson's most aggressive writing. Lloyd George is shown as a fountain of rhetorical evasiveness; the famous dean of St Paul's, Dean Inge, is reduced to 'a class-prejudiced clergyman'; and as for that jack-in-the-box of political careerism, Winston Churchill, Pearson predicted that 'nothing short of death will prevent Winston from becoming Prime Minister of the country for which he has so nobly sacrificed all his principles'. In an age of acerbic new journalism, Pearson was encouraged to come up with more of these aggressive opinions, and congratulated by W. A. Darlington in the *Daily Telegraph* on having 'mixed with his ink a touch of vitriol'.

And there was another temptation. Some reviewers of *Modern Men and Mummers*, while praising Pearson as a good reporter of other men's words, added that he possessed no good words of his own. Here was a challenge he had to answer. He did so by inventing an amusing conversation between G. K. Chesterton and Bernard Shaw. This was published in Middleton Murry's *The Adelphi* in 1923, and Pearson was gratified to see it taken up by several American and British journals as if it were a verbatim account and not a parody – it was even translated into Polish and printed in full by a leading Warsaw newspaper. The joke could hardly have worked better or gone further. Twenty-five years later it was to appear in Louis Biancolli's *The Book of Great Conversations* and, more recently still, treated as important source material in a scholarly volume by a hapless American academic. Pearson was encouraged in his belief that the biographer and historian are justified in using invention whenever it can 'improve on fact'. He had been sailing between fiction and non-fiction for several years. With *The Whispering Gallery* he set a bolder course.

One reason for writing this book was the need to make money. *Modern Men and Mummers* had put his stage career in jeopardy, and after his contract with *John Bull* came to an end, he looked desperately for a new source of income. John Lane at the Bodley Head was to offer him an advance on royalties of £250 – equivalent to about £7,000 at the end of the century.

But there were other motives too. *The Whispering Gallery* is a counter-attack on those figures of authority – his rather bullying father, sadistic schoolmasters, numskull army officers – who had made his life intermittently wreched and exacerbated his fits of temper. These moments of temper are reflected in what his friend Hugh Kingsmill was to call his 'sunstroke style'. Pearson himself seems to have recognised something of this. Though careful not to mention *The Whispering Gallery* by name in his reminiscences *Thinking it Over* (it never appeared among his publications listed in *Who's Who*), he suggests that 'a good deal of irritation I experienced in the war' seeped into the book.

But there was a good deal of fun too. It was irresistible being able to call Asquith, the ex-prime minister, 'an old woman in trousers' and attribute the phrase to Lord Northcliffe, or write of Margot Asquith that 'she must be in the swim, even at the risk of being out of her depths'. He had the freedom to invent conversations that read as if they were scenes from plays, to try out all sorts of juvenile epigrams and paradoxes – and if they didn't work, then the failure was apparently other people's. It was almost worth failing, and giving them the bluntest language. He also had the freedom to use rumour and speculation as if it were fact. We learn that Lord Randolph Churchill had tertiary syphilis, and that the Prince of Wales (later Edward VIII) was embittered by falling in love with someone he couldn't marry. 'I wonder what they [the newspapers] would say if I were to take their advice and marry according to my own inclination?' he is made to say – a percipient speculation almost six years before his meeting with Wallis Simpson. Other pages have the merit of taking on the popular press – for example his extraordinarily vitriolic pen portrait of the assassinated Tsar Nicholas II ('if any man deserved his fate, he certainly did') contrasted with the reasonable description of Lenin ('an impersonal kindness, a concrete coldness but an abstract warmth') which was written when the *Daily Mail* and other newspapers were campaigning virulently against Russian communism. His opinion that Germany was responsible for the Great War, stated at a time when liberal thinkers were arguing that she was the victim of the Versailles Treaty, could gain no credence until the work of revisionist German historians forty years later. Pearson was like a boy with a hammer, hitting all over the place, sometimes with accuracy, sometimes with unnecessary cruelty. He did not mean to hurt people's feelings, he later explained, so much as to relieve his own, and he came to see the book as part of his education at the public expense.

The publication of *The Whispering Gallery* was an extraordinary event. John Lane and his fellow directors at the Bodley Head quickly realised the promotional advantage of bringing out the book anonymously, but stipulated that Pearson, who had presented himself as an agent for the anonymous author, reveal his identity to one of the company directors. The person chosen was Allen Lane, later to become celebrated as the founder of Penguin Books. The name Pearson gave him in strict confidence was that of a senior diplomat called Rennell Rodd.

Sir James Rennell Rodd P.C. G.C.B. G.C.M.G. G.C.V.O. K.C.M.G. C.B., soon to be created Lord Rennell of Rodd, was the sort of English establishment figure Pearson particularly disliked. He was a classical scholar, occasional poet, and a professional diplomat who had served in Berlin, Athens and Cairo, been Britain's Envoy Extraordinary and Minister Plenipotentiary to Sweden, and Ambassador to the Court of Italy. At the age of 68 he was preparing to enter parliament as the Conservative member for St Marylebone. At first sight his career, studded with foreign decorations, may have appeared sufficiently various and far-flung for him to have been to all the places and known all the monarchs, emperors, presidents, crown princes and prime ministers who, in the pages of *The Whispering Gallery*, press their confidences upon the anonymous author. Certainly Allen Lane seems to have believed that Rodd was the secret diarist. And yet, even Dr Watson could have spotted that this was impossible. The author reveals that, like Lord Kitchener, he had not been to Oxford; Rodd had gone to Balliol College, Oxford. The diarist lists his recreations as: 'heraldry, wild birds and squash rackets'; Rodd's recreation was fencing. Rodd had never been posted to Washington where Woodrow Wilson unburdens himself to our diarist, or to St Petersburg and Moscow where he observes the frailties of Tsar Nicholas II. The whole reckless, radical and indeed republican tone of *The Whispering Gallery* is quite different from the decorous three volumes of *Social and Diplomatic Memories* which Rodd himself had published between 1922 and 1925. But the Bodley Head directors believed the book would be a bestseller. In his book *God's Apology*, an account of the friendship between Pearson, Kingsmill and Malcolm Muggeridge, Richard Ingrams tells us that review copies were sent out in November 1926 with accompanying slips stating that *The Whispering Gallery* would be in the publisher's view 'one of the most talked-of books of the season'. Lane added: 'We can vouch for the authenticity of the volume as we know the diarist personally.'

The opening chapter of the book is what the *New Statesman* was to call a brilliant and truthful description of the late Lord Northcliffe, founder of the *Daily Mail*, who is shown attempting to bribe our anonymous diarist for secret information. This led immediately to a dramatic attack on the book by the *Daily Mail*. Under a series of outraged headlines — 'A SCANDALOUS FAKE EXPOSED — MONSTROUS ATTACKS ON PUBLIC MEN — REPUDIATIONS BY FIVE CABINET MINISTERS', the paper denounced the book as a reckless invention which imputed 'conscienceless egotism and disgraceful levity' to many honourable British statesmen. It then launched into an editorial exposé. Bosphorus was spelt Bosphorous; General Townshend was robbed of his middle 'h', and the author repeatedly misused the auxiliaries 'will' and 'would', making Joseph Chamberlain say 'I wouldn't be where I am if I had been a gentleman'. The *Daily Mail* commented: 'Those who know Mr Chamberlain and have documents written by him in their possession know that he spoke the King's English.' Elsewhere Lord Robert Cecil was quoted as saying: 'At no time in my life has Lord Balfour ever called me "Robert", nor have I ever smoked a cigar', while Asquith complained that he had never called Lloyd George 'David' or been addressed by him as 'Asquith'. The political conversations were denounced by Winston Churchill as 'pureile in their ignorance'.

The publishers were delighted by this fuss which quickly spread to other newspapers. In an *Observer* leader headed 'Ghouls and Garbage', J. L. Garvin described the author as 'an imposter and a cad' and the book as 'an unscrupulous farrago'. Three editions of *The Whispering Gallery* quickly sold out and John Lane retaliated: 'The book seems to us to ring true ... There is no question of it being withdrawn.'

All this suddenly changed when the *Daily Mail* switched its attack to the 'Disreputable Publisher', accusing John Lane The Bodley Head of being party to a disgusting fraud, and refusing to take advertisements from them for any of their books. What then happened has been described by Richard Ingrams.

'The directors of John Lane were by now rattled. They decided that if anyone was going to carry the can it would have to be Hesketh Pearson ... [They] went down to the *Daily Mail* and denounced Hesketh Pearson as the villain of the piece ... and acknowledged that they had been the victims of "a most ingenious hoax" ...

'The next day all Hell was let loose on the wretched Pearson. Under the heading "A case for the Public Prosecutor" the *Daily Mail* thundered: "... Messrs John Lane have been victims of one of the most impudent literary forgeries on record ... The next step in this sordid affair lies with the public prosecutor".'

A former Lord Chancellor, Lord Birkenhead, joined in the fray, praising the *Daily Mail* for having performed 'a real and lasting service to the community', and Sir Rennell Rodd himself, whom Allen Lane, breaking his vow of strict confidence, had gone to see, called for 'some action to be taken for the protection of the public'.

The action taken was by John Lane The Bodley Head which, anxious to avoid prosecution itself, withdrew the book from publication and swore an affidavit charging Pearson with attempting to obtain money by false pretences. Pearson himself, who in a paralysis of panic had continued to maintain that Rodd was the author, believing that by doing so he was protecting Allen Lane, had actually repaid the £250 to the publishers before the criminal charge was laid and could therefore logically be accused only of an attempted fraud. His biographer Ian Hunter records that on November 25 he returned to London from an acting engagement in Cardiff pursued all the way by photographers and reporters, who continued over the weeks to besiege him.

'A warrant had been issued for his arrest and he surrendered himself into custody at Marlborough Street Police Court. His brother-in-law, Colonel Dane Hamlett, arranged bail of £1000 and took charge of the defence. The case was set down for hearing at London sessions. Sir Patrick Hastings, a man devoted to the theatre and the ablest barrister of his day, was briefed for the defence.'

Friends and colleagues from the stage and literary communities rallied to his side, and many unknown people sent sympathetic messages. But everyone advised him to plead guilty. Bernard Shaw wrote that his choice was 'between the heaviest sentence the court can give him and a lenient one. If he puts up a defence he will get the heavy sentence ... but if he pleads guilty and throws himself on the mercy of the court, apologising to Sir R.R. and the Lane Firm ... he may get off lightly'. Pearson's family suggested he should plead for mitigation on the grounds of insanity brought on by his head wound in Mesopotamia, and only Frank Harris, the notorious author of *My Life and Loves*, writing from the south of France, advised him to claim that memoirs are a well-known form of fiction, 'Say that a widely-known literary man told you this. It will make the court laugh.'

On the evening before the trial at the London Sessions on 26 January 1927, Patrick Hastings called Pearson to his Temple chambers and advised him to plead guilty. If he did so he was likely to be bound over. But if he was found guilty by the jury he would get up to six months' imprisonment. But Pearson was determined not to capitulate to what he considered an unfounded accusation. He had been guilty of folly, but was not a criminal. Had he really wanted to fool the publishers, he would have chosen a dead diplomat as the secret author. He refused to apologise to people who were attempting to get to shore by pushing him off the raft. Patrick Hastings promised to do all he could to obtain a verdict in his favour, and the following morning went on the attack in court, asking Allen Lane to compare *The Whispering Gallery*, which contained nothing lubricious, with other books on their list.

Allen Lane refused to read out passages from Ovid's *Art of Love* and Apuleius's *Golden Ass*, though at the same time denying they were obscene books. The erotic illustrations to these and other books (the Bodley Head had also published a modern anonymous novel purporting to be 'letters from a lady to the captain of a ship') were passed round the gentlemen, but not the two ladies, of the jury, and regarded by the judge through the fingers of a hand with which, in horror, he covered his face.

When Pearson was called to the witness box, prosecuting counsel, Sir Henry Curtis-Bennett, asked him why he had chosen Rodd's name. 'I think it was because I couldn't think of anyone less likely to have written the book', he replied. 'So you started the lie taking the most unlikely person in your view?' he was asked. 'Yes, to show that it was a lie.' 'Do you realise what you are saying?' Pearson repeated that he had admitted lying and would save the prosecutor's breath by confessing to double the number of lies with which he was being taxed – at which point, Pearson having confessed that he had been 'mad', the prosecuting counsel sat down.

The jury was out for less than half an hour before returning a verdict of not guilty. At the celebration in a pub near by, several members of the jury told him that his engaging candour had won them over. Pearson himself later attributed the avalanche of publicity that had engulfed the book and himself to one of those outbreaks of mania due 'not to their ostensible cause, but to the annoyance with life felt by the majority of people, whose accumulated disappointments generate resentment, the expression of which is held in check by conventions and circumstances until released by the creation of a public scapegoat, on whom they can vent their baffled fury and join in the hue and cry without forfeiting their social respectability. I had read of these epidemics in the cases of Byron, Oscar Wilde, Parnell and Dreyfus ... I naturally warm towards scapegoats. But it is not pleasant to be one, and I did not think it funny at the time.'

The epidemic ended as quickly as it began. The publishers, realising they had not behaved well, handed over his royalties from the book, which, together with his American royalties, enabled him to reimburse those who had paid for his defence. But he had not escaped without damage. No British publisher would look at his work for more than three years, and the next book 'by the author of *The Whispering Gallery*', a series of biographical discourses called *Ventilations*, which argues the case for introducing fiction into biography to reach an 'essential truth', was only published in the United States. Until 1931, Pearson earned most of his income from the stage, one of his most successful roles being the villain in a melodrama called *The Acquittal*.

Pearson was to rebuild his career in the 1930s, beginning with a Life of his forebear, the physician Erasmus Darwin, which was proclaimed in a leading article in the *Times Literary Supplement* as 'one of the models of sensible ancestor-worship'. By this time he had changed his mind on biographical methodology. 'It is only after one has experienced the labour and anxiety of searching for the truth that one knows how to value it.'

The Whispering Gallery is a curiosity, not simply on account of its short dramatic history, but also because it may now be seen as a primitive experiment to extend the frontiers of biography. This is not a one-book cul-de-sac, but part of a long intermittent and uncertain road continually being explored by biographers. It has led to several celebrated experiments, from the conversations staged by Peter Ackroyd in his *Dickens* to the passages of nineteenth-century pastiche inserted by Andrew Motion into *Wainwright the Poisoner*, for which Hesketh Pearson's book stands as a distant, weather-beaten signpost.

PREFACE

FIRST, a few words about myself. Among the diplomats of Europe my name is a household word. I say this in no boastful spirit. It just happens to be so. The general public, too, have seen my name in print often enough, but it probably means no more to them than, let us say, the name of a tooth-paste.

During the last thirty years my work in the diplomatic service has put me into close touch with most of the prominent men in Europe. I have met them, to a great extent, in circumstances of privacy, when they have not been in the public gaze—when, in fact, they have been most themselves. And I have been amazed at the strange lack of first-hand, authentic portraiture of these national figures in the volumes that have glutted the book-market of late years under the heading of " Memoirs," of " Pen-Portraits," and of " Autobiography ".

Here, in my work, you shall see these men faithfully drawn for the first time. I have no desire to be malicious, no desire to flatter. I merely wish to tell the truth, as I see it, without fear and with no hope of favour. The job must be done by someone, and I doubt if anyone has had better opportunities for close observation than myself. Certainly no one, having had such opportunities, is likely to make such use of them as I have done here.

For various reasons I have remained anonymous. This will not impose upon anyone " in the know," but certain social and family considerations have forced me to adopt such a course, and from the point of view of the Corps to which I belonged it seemed advisable.

The entire book, as will appear, has been compiled from a diary which I have kept pretty consistently ever since I reached the age of twenty-one. The diary itself could not be published as it stands ; and, moreover, the grouping together of personalities and incidents in their present form seemed to me a more satisfactory method of dealing with my material than giving it to the public as a series of abbreviated entries from a diary. Besides, I do not wish to give too much away, and only by eliminating certain dates and places can I leave people guessing. Not that I wish to mystify the general reader, but I am anxious to keep a few cards up my sleeve in case of contradiction by certain living politicians or the relatives of the dead who have been dealt with in my book.

As to the title, a word is perhaps needful. To move in high social or diplomatic circles is to live in a whispering gallery. No secret can be breathed without the startling reverberation of rumour from an unexpected quarter. The secrets I have breathed in these pages have already found their echo in the circles of hearsay, an echo which distorts the words that were actually spoken and alters the very character of the speaker.

In this chronicle I have recaptured the words and sometimes even the moods of the speakers ; and if my record remains a whispering gallery, it is chiefly so because some of the disclosures should only be spoken in a whisper, but partly also because the accents reach us from the past, down the long corridor of Time.

THE WHISPERING GALLERY

THE WHISPERING GALLERY

CHAPTER I

THE NAPOLEON OF FLEET STREET

Lord Northcliffe.

ABOUT ten years after the commencement of my diplomatic career I came into touch with the Press in a somewhat dramatic fashion. I was sitting one evening in my lodgings in Westminster, " getting up " the details of an affair that was then absorbing the attention of half the Foreign Offices in Europe, when my landlady came into the room and said a gentleman wanted to see me on urgent private business. Thinking it might be one of my clerks from the office—no one else could possibly want me on urgent or private business, nor did anyone outside my immediate circle of friends know my address—I told her to send him up.

There entered, in a minute, a tall, fair man, with light eyelashes and a ginger moustache, whom I didn't know from Adam. He seemed vaguely uneasy, and when I asked him to sit down he remained standing. At last he broke out with :

" I am a newspaper representative."

I assured him that I was duly impressed and again begged him to be seated. This time he obliged me, but during the whole of our interview he sat on the edge of the chair, twirling and pinching his hat as if in a state of acute mental discomfort.

" Now what can I do for you ? " I asked.

" Nothing for me, sir," he answered, " but for my chief."

" And who may your chief be ? " I queried.

" Lord Northcliffe," he replied.

(I might mention here that I always made verbatim reports of any conversations that struck me at the time as interesting. I did so in nearly every case immediately after their occurrence, while they were still fresh in my memory, which will account for the general accuracy of all the episodes I relate.)

At the mention of that nobleman's name I pricked up my ears, as you may guess, and awaited what followed with interest.

" Go on," I said.

It took him a long time to come to the point. At first he thought it necessary to explain the importance of the Harmsworth Press in the general scheme of the universe. But by dint of pressure on my part he eventually got to the cause of his visit.

" Well, sir," he said at last, " it's like this. The chief has heard of you from a friend of his, and he is very interested in you."

" I am flattered," I returned ; " but in that case

why doesn't he do me the honour of calling personally ? "

" Ah, that would hardly do," said my visitor quickly ; " you see, he has a business proposition to make."

I gently urged him to formulate the proposition.

" He wants you to write for him."

I expressed the pleasure it would give me to write for his chief, and added that the subjects on which I believed myself an authority were heraldry, wild birds and squash rackets. He smiled in a wearily indulgent manner and intimated that " the chief" would be more anxious to have my views in other directions.

" Inside stuff is what he's after," said the gentleman with the ginger moustache.

I begged for further enlightenment.

" Well, sir, it's like this "—he always started an explanation in those words—" he would like you to write about your own work."

" A very interesting topic," said I. " I should like to write a history of the diplomatic service, but of course I'd have to get the permission of my superiors."

" Good heavens ! You mustn't do that ! " he exclaimed ; and then, in a lower tone, " You must please treat this matter as strictly confidential."

I urged him to be explicit and tell me exactly what his chief wanted.

" Well, sir, it's like this. You are in a position to know how things are shaping—internationally, I mean—and if you could see your way to tipping us the wink whenever anything really interesting is going on behind the scenes, you'd find it was worth your while."

Those were the very words in which this amazing proposal was first put to me. For a few moments, being comparatively new to the (what shall I call them?) amenities of public life, I lay back in my chair mentally stunned by what I then regarded as a superb impertinence. I now know that these offers are as common as ditch-water, and that they are pretty frequently accepted.

After recovering from the shock, my sense of humour got the better of me and I decided to see the thing through, promising myself an entertaining curtain. Meanwhile the ginger moustache was being pulled with such vigour that in order to save its shape I put my visitor at his ease.

" A very intriguing proposition," I commented; "but I should like to have the whole arrangement made clear by Lord Northcliffe himself. Besides, I could hardly enter into an agreement on a matter of such vital importance with anyone less than the principal. When could I see him ? "

The representative of the Harmsworth Press got on his feet so suddenly that he knocked over the chair on which he had been sitting. Having apologized for his clumsiness and set it on its legs, he thanked me for my " courtesy," said I would probably hear from " the chief " to-morrow, and held out his hand. I wished him good-night and saw him off the premises.

Next day I received a wire : " Shall be alone to-night. Will you dine with me at my house ? Seven o'clock. Northcliffe." I wired back that I should be delighted ; and as Big Ben was striking the hour I was pressing his lordship's front-door bell.

The man, I must say, surprised me. All through dinner he was the quintessence of charm. His conversation was informative without being boring and anecdotal without being commonplace. I mean that he had the art of telling one things without appearing to do so, and all his stories illuminated the characters of the people about whom he told them.

I noticed one thing about him very shortly after our first handshake. He was far too anxious to make a good impression. His smile, which was frequent was often forced ; and the softer notes of his voice seemed to me to be " put on " for the occasion. There was also just a little too much of " my dear fellow " about his method of addressing me.

Some of his comments on the leading people of the day were of extraordinary interest to me, because they came naturally through ordinary conversational channels, and, being impromptu, were probably honest.

Balfour he described as " a marionette who has command over his own wires—a man whom one cannot tempt because he has no temptations—a trifler who plays with politics because the game mildly amuses him—a fellow of parts and no passions."

He dismissed Joseph Chamberlain in a phrase or two : " Damned clever devil ! Ought to be Prime Minister. Not if I can help it, though, Too much like me—one half of me, I mean."

And this was his estimate of King Edward VII : " The greatest monarch we've ever had—on a race-course. Only thank God he doesn't meddle in politics like his mother ! I had half-an-hour's chat with him once and in a very tactful manner he suggested that newspapers should not attack ministers of the Crown. I evaded the issue. He returned to it. So I said ; ' That, sir, is the chief function of modern journalism.' ' Indeed ? ' he said. ' I thought its *chief* function was to collect and distribute news.' I bowed and was silent, not wishing to pursue the topic. He continued : ' An attack on a minister of the Crown might be construed into an attack on the Crown itself ' ' No, sir,' I retorted. ' A newspaper, like a politician, is the servant of the public. It criticises the public actions of the public servants. The Crown is not nowadays represented by the policy, but only by the persons, of its ministers. We attack the policy.' Not bad, that, eh ? Teddie smiled and said : ' An admirable stroke. You are more dangerous than I thought you were—which means, I hope, more valuable.' Then he changed the subject."

After dinner we adjourned to Northcliffe's study

where coffee, liqueurs and cigars were brought. Suddenly I noticed that he began to get very fidgety. He left his armchair and paced several times up and down the room, throwing scraps of conversation at me as he did so in a nervous staccato way that made me feel quite uncomfortable :

" I can't get anything new nowadays . . . . Not one of my people has an ounce of imagination . . . . Damned fools ! . . . . Damned fools ! . . . . I've digested all the novelty possible in the newspaper world . . . . And spewed it out . . . . Nothing left to spew . . . . Idiots ! . . . . Not an ounce of brains between the lot of 'em . . . . Bloody fatheads ! . . . . . What ? "

He shouted the last word at me with such force that I nearly ruined an admirable cigar by biting off half-an-inch. However, I managed to maintain a reasonable appearance of calmness, and he went on :

" That's why I'm prepared to pay for the right sort of stuff. You know the kind—wheels within wheels—submarine currents—and what-not. I'm sick of the stuff I get from the stables. I want it straight from the horse's mouth. And, what's more, I'll pay for it ! Through the nose, if need be. But no hankey-pankey. It's the bona-fide goods I'm after . . . . See ? "

I was half prepared for the final bark, though I didn't come through it quite unscathed. It was my tongue, not the cigar, that suffered this time. In spite of the admirable dinner and the nectareal old

brandy at my side, my host's present tactics were
beginning to jar upon my keyed-up nerves. However, I thought it best to give him as much rein as
he wanted, and off he went shortly in another gallop :
"Take this silly Russian business. What's at the
back of it ? We're asking for trouble—and we'll get
it. But I could save the situation if I had the facts.
That's where I'm cornered. No facts. No data.
Nothing to go on. Give me the facts and I can
promise the fireworks. My boobies can write well
enough—damn them!—though that's about all they
can do. And it's all in the public interest. Don't
forget that. You'd be serving your country far more
efficaciously than you're doing it now . . . . I tell
you if I can't get the stuff from you, there are others.
It'll be got somehow, if I have to bribe old ———
for it. . . . Well ? "

Though the last word was almost shouted in my
ear, I survived it with an effort. By this time he had
worked himself up into an extraordinary state. He
was stamping the floor, pounding on the various
articles of furniture and smiting the palms of his
hands. I decided that the time had come for me to
speak. On the face of it his next outbreak might
easily have culminated in a personal assault.

"What is it you are asking me to do ? " I inquired.

For several seconds there was a stony silence. He
came to anchor on the hearthrug and stood there
staring down as though I was a being from another
sphere, fossilized for his particular benefit.

"I thought it was all arranged," he said at last.

"Thought *what* was all arranged?" I countered.

"That you were to give me the inside stuff I want."

"But what *do* you want?"

"Didn't he tell you?"

"No."

"Then what the devil——!" He pulled himself up there and began whistling quietly, still keeping his eyes glued to mine.

"I thought," he pursued after a while, "it was merely a question of an agreement as to terms."

Another long silence, during which I could tell by the concentrated expression in his eyes that he was doing some pretty hard thinking. Then a very strange thing happened, for which I have never been able to account. He pointed to the whiskey at my side, said "Help yourself," subsided into an armchair facing me, and started telling me stories of his early life.

His whole manner altered. Once again he became the charming host, all smiles and suavity. Following so quickly upon the preceding scene, his behaviour completely nonplussed me, and not one of the stories he told took root in my consciousness. I must have sat there literally gaping at him for an hour or more.

One thing, however, did not escape me. About a minute before we were interrupted, I noticed his hand drop to a spot somewhere below the arm of his chair. The action was deliberate, not accidental—

that I could swear. And shortly afterwards there was a knock at the door. A male servant entered and informed his lordship that " Mr. Cripps " had called on important business.

My host rose, apologized for having to finish our "interesting chat," and expressed his delight at having made my acquaintance, which he hoped to renew at the first opportunity. He shook my hand warmly, came with me into the hall, and with a farewell word walked rapidly back into his study.

He had beaten me at my own game. There could be no doubt about that. But *how* he had managed to scent danger beats me to this day. I met him at least three more times. On each occasion he was studiously polite and formal, but nothing of interest passed between us.

No one has so far summarized the essential features of his character, so I will attempt to do it here.

By the large majority of his employees he was dreaded. He was utterly undependable. At one moment nothing could be too good for someone he had taken a fancy to ; at another moment nothing could be too bad. He loved flattery, and those who laid it on with a trowel were his favourites. He would ask the most impossible things of his subordinates and treat them w th unreasonable irritab lity when they failed to execute his incredible commands.

Like everyone else in the world he had his good points. He was a delightful host. He raised the scale of wages throughout the world of British journalism. And he was one of the twenty odd million people in these islands who helped to win the war against Germany. But he domineered over the people who worked for him ; and when they refused to toe the line any longer, they had to go.

That, for the first time, is the truth about Lord Northcliffe. Perhaps I ought in fairness to add that he loved a romp with the children—though it was quite a different sort of romp from that which he daily enjoyed with the grown-up children of Carmelite House !

CHAPTER II

WARRIORS

Lord Kitchener, Lord Roberts, Sir Redvers Buller, Sir John French, Marshal Joffre, Townsend of Kut.

§1

BARRING the members of my own profession, I have come into contact with more famous politicians than the notable people in any other walk of life. But quite a few warriors swam into my ken, and of some of these I will now write. The majority of my military acquaintances were, I found, men with very little intelligence outside their profession. Let me give an instance of this.

Early in 1908 I was in India, where I had my first experience of working with Lord Kitchener. About three years before he had quarrelled with Lord Curzon over the question of dual control (civil and military) in the Indian Army. He had won the day and Curzon had gone home. But, although I was positive on the point, nothing could convince him that Curzon's attitude was not actuated by any other motive than vanity.

"The man's a gilded popinjay," said Kitchener

over and over again. And another sentence was constantly in his mouth : " He'll never forgive me for clipping his wings. He thinks I want his job."

One day I decided to argue the matter out with him. I was lunching with him alone. Over our cigars I put the case from Curzon's point of view before him. Kitchener blinked at some of my more cogent passages, but kept silent until I had done. Then he took the cigar out of his mouth, turned towards me, and said with a ponderous solemnity :

" Your argument is far too convincing to be true."

I tried to press the matter home, but he waved it aside :

" It won't do," he said ; " I have frequently known my reasoning powers to fail, never my instincts. This is an instinct. The fight has been Oxford v. Woolwich. It isn't the first time I've made Oxford eat mud—and it won't be the last."

He made this statement with such relish that I felt quite thankful I hadn't been to Oxford. But I came away with the impression that Kitchener's intelligence was hardly of the first order.

I could never quite make him out. Sometimes he was so communicative as to be garrulous. Other times he wouldn't open his mouth for hours at a stretch. On the subject of " antiques," old china, porcelain, etc., he'd chatter away until everyone else yawned. Switch him on to another topic, and he'd be the first to yawn.

For the staple subject of conversation at mess—

women—he had little or no use, even going so far as to say on one occasion that " the majority of men only talk about women because they'd be thought unmanly if they didn't ! "

Once I was present during a deliciously typical incident. Kitchener never cared a damn for literature. He read books for information, seldom for pleasure. Consequently, whenever the subject arose he simply sank into himself and remained mute. Someone was discussing Shakespeare. The ball of talk was tossed from one to another until Morley noticed that Kitchener was brooding abstractedly. With a certain amount of tactful insistence he contrived to bring him back into the conversation. Having succeeded, at any rate, in getting the soldier's eyes off the ceiling and on to the table, Morley asked him what he honestly thought about Shakespeare. There was a dead silence. Kitchener looked from one eager face to another. Then his glance came to rest on John Morley's beaming countenance. At last :

" Shakespeare ? " he drawled ; " Shakespeare ? " A pause. Then : " Isn't that the fellow who talked about the ' pride, pomp and circumstance of glorious war ' ? "

The subject was allowed to drop. . . .

The real tragedy of Kitchener has never, I think, been told. It was this : he pined for human affection, but was never able to inspire it. As 'a result, he was really indifferent to life ; and he had no sense whatever of the value of human life. The appalling massacre of Omdurman I once heard him describe as " a great relief to the feelings." I was revolted at the time, but afterwards I began to understand. He had scented a kindred spirit in Gordon, and he hated these people for murdering him. It so happened that his method of squaring the account was also his country's method. So in every sense of the word it was " a great relief to the feelings."

It is, I suppose, only natural that a professional soldier can best express his soul in the shedding of blood, and Kitchener certainly had no objection to killing as a trade ; but his traditional hardness was chiefly, as I have said, caused by his friendlessness. He distrusted most people, and such as might have come to like him were repelled by his aloofness. He was one of the world's " solitaries," never feeling at ease among a number of people ; and because he was capable only of deep affection or of utter indifference, he had no circle of everyday friends.

In short he was the type of man who will always be an alien in England—which is a country of frigid friendships. And how he hated what he called the "club-frequenting politicians " ! Once, when he was in a bitter mood, I asked if anything could make him really happy.

" Yes," he said with surprising promptness." First secure a full sitting of the House of Commons, then bar and bolt all the exits and entrances to it except one ; next place me with half a dozen men and a couple of machine guns at that one, and finally set fire to the building. I think I could promise you a smile of satisfaction at the conclusion of the entertainment."

I was sorry for Kitchener. All his life he fought a hard battle against misunderstanding—and he himself led the forces on the opposing side. . . .

§2

Could any two characters have been more at variance than those of Kitchener and Roberts ? There was something monumentally slow and unresponsive about the former ; but the latter was quick, adaptable, mercurial and easy-going. I was present at a meeting between these two warriors and was sensible enough to jot down a minute of their conversation. Reading it now I cannot help feeling that it's an extraordinary commentary on the characters of the two men. This is the fragment that I preserved:

Rob : The Germans would have the pick of the English coast to land on.

Kit : What would our navy be doing ?

Rob : Keeping a decent look-out over 100 miles of coast-line, leaving the remaining 600 fair game to the marauders.

Kit : Not so easy as you think. A fleet of transports would hardly reach our coasts without being noticed by someone.

Rob : At night-time ?

Kit : (*musing*) H'm.

Rob : Besides, they needn't keep together.

Kit : H'm.

Rob : And they could land troops at different places.

Kit : H'm.

Rob : Which would cause a panic.

Kit : H'm.

Rob : So you see !

Kit : (*after a long pause*) They wouldn't dare. They haven't the initiative, the—the imagination—

Rob : You mean *we* haven't the imagination.

Kit : I don't follow you.

Rob : We haven't the imagination to credit them with the imagination.

Kit : Oh !

Rob : Well, don't you agree ?

Kit : (*stolidly*) No.

" Bobs " chucked it after that. But I noticed a sort of indulgent gleam of merriment in his eyes which as good as said : " The dear fellow can't help being a silly ass ! "

Lord Roberts was a most likeable fellow. No one could quarrel with him for long, simply because he refused to keep it up. He never bore malice, and though he often said a thing he didn't mean in the heat of the moment, he always took the first opportunity to retract it. I remember an instance of this.

General Buller had apparently been behaving in a somewhat irascible manner and had said something that had seriously offended " Bobs". As far as I can remember, it was to the effect that he (Buller) had done all the dirty work in the South African war and had " prepared the way for the Lord," who got all the credit as well as the cash.

Roberts, in a moment of quite natural exasperation, said : " I wonder how many drinks went to that epigram ? Buller will never forgive me for remaining strictly sober."

The hearty laughter that greeted this remark instantly made Roberts conscious of his indiscretion and conscious, too, of his uncharitableness. Almost at once he seized a chance to correct the impression he had made :

" I envy some men their honest and healthy enjoyment of life," he said : " Buller for instance. What a splendid fellow ! Worshipped by his men—and rightly so. He often says things he doesn't mean— but then, so do we all."

A handsome recantation ; and the dear old boy meant it too . . . .

§3

I didn't know Sir Redvers Buller very well, and the few times I met him he always struck me as boorish and off-hand. But that can hardly be called a fair test, because he hated what he called my "tribe"—meaning diplomats generally. The mere fact that it was our profession to be tactful was proof-positive to him that we were a lot of " damned liars". I must admit that he himself was a model of honesty and plain-speaking—rather too much so for some

people.   He detested " beating about the bush " and
preferred the brutal truth to the plain truth.   I mean
he'd never accuse a man of not being a gentleman ;
he'd tell him right out that he was a " bloody cad".

On one point there can be no two opinions.
Among the soldiers Buller was the most popular
General we have ever put into the field.   The popularity of " Bobs " couldn't be compared with that of
Buller.   He was simply worshipped by the Tommies.
And chiefly for two reasons.   Firstly, his personal
courage.   He'd never ask a man to do what he
wouldn't prefer to do himself.   Secondly (and of
greater importance) his care of the men under his
command.   He looked after their rations and general
comfort as no commanding officer ever did before
or since him.   And Tommy quite rightly adores the
man who fills his belly.

Buller's downrightness was the cause of his down-
fall.   He blurted out things in public that were better
left unsaid.   But he coined his own epitaph within
a few weeks of his death.   Speaking to a friend of
mine, he used these words : " You recall Tennyson's
lines—' Theirs not to reason why, Theirs but to do
do or die ' ?   Well, I made the mistake of doing or
dying, but at the same time why-ing. . . ."

§4

Sir John French (as he was called when I knew
him best) was a very different type.   A sensitive,

nervous, temperamental fellow, who never spoke out unless he got " rattled " and then said far too much. Always very popular in polite circles, he was what is commonly termed " a lady's man". He loved the society of women and became moody and fretful whenever he was called upon to endure their absence for any length of time.

In certain respects he was quite like a child. If anything upset him seriously, he would become hysterical. After which, unless he was petted, he would sulk for an indefinite period.

I personally liked him enormously. That was because I got on well with him ; though I quite sympathized with those whom he irritated. The great thing was to keep him calm, smooth him down the right way, never get on his nerves by pursuing a topic he resented. Because the moment he got to boiling-point, both reason and commonsense went flying to the winds as (in the coloured language of an emphatic epoch) Sir John took a series of "headers" off the deep-end. Such a statement should be fortified by fact—so here goes.

There was a men's dinner-party in Curzon Street just before the war. French was there, and in the course of the meal he worked himself up into a very excited condition over the recent happenings in Ireland. Unfortunately the man sitting opposite him was doing the one thing that infuriated Sir John more than anything else in the world—with an acid politeness he was practically contradicting everything the well-known soldier was saying. To nearly every statement he shook his head and remarked : "I doubt it."

Of course the matter was at that time highly controversial, and French should never have opened it—if he did—still less have pursued it when he came up against opposition. But he was spurred on against his calmer self by the aggravating "I doubt it" from the other side of the table.

Eventually, after one of these maddening repetitions, he broke off, and leaning over towards his antagonist said in a voice pent with passion :

"If you doubt it, you are an ignorant idiot, sir."

The other smiled across at him indulgently and said : "I doubt it."

That finished French. Shaking with rage, he told the doubter—in a series of jerky, clipped, but very forceful phrases—exactly what he would like to do to him. Among other items in the catalogue of hostile acts was that of rubbing his nose in the dirt.

Of course everyone present did the only possible thing, and an immense buzz of conversation was set up to drown the "scene". Each person suddenly thought of something he was bursting to tell his fellow, and for a while there was a regular hubbub of verbal evacuation. Then, as so often happens after a spurt of indiscriminate eloquence, there was a deathly silence. Even Sir John was quelled by it.

But in the uncomfortable void thus created, a still, small voice was heard to say : " I doubt it."

French literally went purple. The rest of the party, in their apoplectic efforts to stifle laughter, nearly copied him. The situation was saved by our host, who with much tact and adroitness drew French into the conversation that had been going on at the top of the table.

To this scene I can add a postscript. The man whose doubts nearly wrecked the dinner-party, then an Under-Secretary of State, was largely responsible at a later date for the supersession of French during the war. No object can be gained by stirring up the mud of those days, so I suppress his name. . . .

§5

French, by the way, simply adored Marshal Joffre —in so many ways his exact opposite. A chapter on Joffre could not explain his character so vividly as one remark he made about French. " A charming man—quite charming," he said to a colleague, " but he suffers terribly, poor dear, from what you call the wind-up."

No one ever suffered less from wind-up than " Papa " Joffre, whose placidity under the most terrifying conditions was well-nigh inhuman. Once a friend expostulated with him for taking a snooze during an action that might have decided the fate of Europe. Joffre simply replied :

" Would you have me stride up and down the room knocking my head at intervals against the wall to keep awake ? "

But I know more of Joffre from others than from personal intercourse, so I will leave him to those others.   He is well worth painting at full length. . .

§6

I have often thought that the man who studies a thing at first-hand is the last man to be relied on. This truth (as I think it) was never better exemplified that in the later career of General Townsend.   Of course some people—very few—are able to control their impulses of admiration or affection or contempt or hatred.   But wherever there is predisposition or prejudice, the " man on the spot " can never be trusted.

Townsend loved the Turks—by which I mean that he loved the few choice specimens whose job it was to butter him up—and therefore he should not have been trusted within a million miles of them.   He honestly believed in the brutes ; and so we were treated to the astounding and monstrous sight of an English commander basking on the banks of the Bosphorous in every imaginable condition of pampered luxury, while his men were beaten and starved to death, under every conceivable circumstance of horror and humiliation, in the loathsome khans and pestilent plains of Upper Mesopotamia.

THE WHISPERING GALLERY

It would be impossible to parallel the crime of Kut in the annals of war. I have heard a man who was through one of its minor phases as well as the retreat from Mons refer to the latter as a Sunday school picnic in comparison. The language that could do justice to its worst phases has not yet been invented ; and in any case no one has come through all its horrors alive and sane.

Time and again (I know this from inside sources) Townsend was implored by Americans and other neutrals of that time to intercede with the Turkish authorities on behalf of his tortured troops. He refused absolutely to believe the stories of their hideous plight that poured in upon him from every side. In effect he answered all the appeals with : "Impossible ! The Turks have given me their word. The Turks are gentlemen."

He hadn't even the intelligence to grasp that the picturesque action of the Turkish commander in permitting him to keep his sword proved nothing but that the Turks were cute enough to perceive he might be useful to them. Which, by the way, he was. Being a soldier—and, within limits, a very efficient one—he contented himself with the observation that the Turks fought like gentlemen (because they were too lazy to fight in any other way), and he remained to the end quite convinced that anyone who said anything against them was a liar.

So, you see, he wasn't in any sense a heartless knave. He was a simple, upright, trusting English

gentleman—and of course a born fool. His men
were the victims of his integrity. And a million
times throughout those hellish days they must have
lifted impotent hands to a brazen heaven and cursed
the fate that gave them a General who was gentleman
enough to trust their enemies instead of a leader
who was cad enough to distrust everyone.

Picture to yourself, then, the arrival of this ingenuous soul on his native shore, shortly after a war
in which he had fought with no little distinction.
See his blank look of amazement when, instead of a
decorated harbour and a civic reception, he is met
by two or three persons of dolorous air and deprecatory mien. The poor fellow is visibly shocked and
—yes, I am sure of it—startled. Advancing nervously
towards us he shakes hands, first with an old friend
or two, then with me. There is emotion in his voice
and—am I wrong ?—a tear in his eye.

I stand aside while he greets his intimates, for I
am only here officially. He speaks with real difficulty,
a gulp or two choking his utterance, and he looks
expectantly now and then over their shoulders, as
though hoping for . . . . what ?

At last he breaks away from his companions and
comes over to me.

" Kind of you to come," he says. But I extract
the rest from my diary :

ME : A duty and a privilege, General.

T : Tell me ; am I not expected so soon ?

ME : We knew of your arrival to-day.

T :   Then——? (*He looks round wonderingly*).

ME : Yes, I think that there has been a misunderstanding.

T :   Misunderstanding ?

ME : Yes. (*A long pause.*)

T :   Then what I heard was true.

ME : Surely you must have known——

T :   Must have known that I couldn't expect gratitude ?—yes.

ME : I didn't mean that.

T :   I know. What you meant was that they've got their knife into me—because I haven't toadied enough, I suppose.

ME : Hardly that, either.

T :   No ? Then you think they are dying to do me justice ?

ME : Well——

T :   Don't be an idiot, man ! You know as well as I do that that swine —— and that super-swine —— have done their best to discredit me. They've done nothing but lie, and lie, and lie ! When I couldn't answer back, too. The scum !

ME : Well, you must admit, General, that your capitulation was a bit desperate. The men came out of it badly. Unpleasant reports have reached us, you know. There's hardly a survivor who wouldn't rather have been killed in Kut among his fellows than have survived outside it among the Turks.

T : Yes, so they say now. But at the time they were as eager as I was to chuck up the sponge. What would you have had me do ? Look on, wringing my hands impotently, while over half my force were gasping out their lives in a vain effort to overcome dysentery, malaria, wounds and starvation—not to speak of the enemy? The thing was impossible,impracticable,unthinkable. Not a single civilized commander in the world would have held out a minute longer than I did against such appalling odds. It would have been absolute suicide, and I would have been rightly blamed. Your armchair critics ought to have the decency——

Me: Forgive me, but I am not criticizing you. I am merely voicing the general feeling.

T : The politician's feeling, you mean.

Me : Well, if you like it, the politician's feeling.

T : The men who have achieved fame by the efforts of others, of the soldiers who have done the dirty work.

Me : Perhaps.

T : The reflectors of a glory that is not their own.

Me : I dare say. (*A pause.*)

T : Then may I ask what you or they would have done in my place ?

Me : It isn't what you did. It is what you left undone. Since you force me to act as public prosecutor—a job I detest—will you answer me one question ?

T : As many as you like.

ME : Why did you *leave* your men ?

T : Because I believed I could be of more use to them in Constantinople.

ME : That, if you will forgive me saying so, was your cardinal error.

T : It may have been. But how could I tell ? You expect me to be infallible.

ME : Not infallible, General, only human. Had you remained with them, the Turks would not have dared to treat them as they did.

T : It has been exaggerated.

ME : Has it ?

T : (*sarcastically*) Perhaps you expected the Turks to give them all the home comforts they were denied in the Service ?

ME : No, I would have expected the Turks to behave exactly as they did behave.

T : (*after a pause*) I will go to the root of this and clear myself.

ME : I am glad to hear you say so, General.

T : But I see how it is. They hate me at head-quarters. My career is finished ; and whatever I say will be used in evidence against me. That's the way of the politicians. Fortunately it is not the way of posterity.

I wonder, but I do not speak. He rejoins his friends, and we all march off a little disconsolately. . . .

CHAPTER III

EMPIRE-BUILDERS

Cecil Rhodes, Joseph Chamberlain.

§1

NEVER can I forget my first meeting with Cecil Rhodes. It was at a diplomatic function in Princes Gate. The man was unbearably rude.

"Another of these carpet-slippered bastards ! " was his perfectly audible " aside " as I was introduced to him.

Our host tried to cover up the faux pas by clearing his throat with unnatural vehemence and remarking in a strained and strident voice that I was shortly going to visit South Africa.

" Is he ? " said Rhodes, eyeing me with much disfavour. "Is he indeed ? Good. He'll probably die there. It's no place for carpet-slippers."

I was slightly in the dark as to the connection between carpet-slippers and the diplomatic service, so I requested the favour of an explanation.

" One can't hear you coming and one can't hear you going," spat out Rhodes (it is the only way I

can describe his unpleasant manner of speech).
" Why the devil can't you warn us of your presence ?
You're neither human in your movements nor animal
in your methods.   You're fish—by God, you are !—
and for preference *cods*."

I reminded him of the saying that hard words
broke no bones.   To which he rejoined :

" That's a fact.   And truth never yet penetrated
the skull of a diplomat."

At this point our host, erroneously supposing that
we were getting on famously, left us to cement the
friendship.   While I was still admiring the unob-
trusive dexterity of his disappearance, Rhodes burst
out with :

" See that old devil in the corner ? "

Thus conjured, I turned my gaze in the direction
he signified and discovered the object of his flattering
remark to be a Countess whose name was a household
word in the land.   My eyes met hers, and I
think under the stress of the moment I coloured.
Nor was I reassured by the complimentary
comment with which Mr. Rhodes noted my
confusion :

" Don't give the blasted show away, Mr. Cod—or
whatever your name is.   That old viper has been
following me about ever since I came to London.
She wants to worm something out of me.   She
probably wants to live with me.   But she reckons
without her dear Cecil.   He'll see himself in hell
before committing his beloved presence to her tender

mercies for ten seconds beyond a ' How de do ? '
So if you value your skin when you come to my
country, you'll fasten yourself on to me until someone
else comes along and unhooks you. I wouldn't be
left alone the prey of that old hag for all the wealth
round her skinny neck."

I was getting used to " dear Cecil" by this time.
Indeed, I was almost beginning to like him in spite
of his somewhat insulting allusions to myself.

" It must be a terrible business avoiding all these
people," I put in.

" Terrible business ? " he cried ; " don't you
believe it ! It's one of the solaces of my otherwise
hectic existence. Why, it's like being a child again
and playing hide-and-seek up and down the staircase.
And when one is run to earth—ah, that's when the
real fun starts ! I call them all the names under the
sun—and, by God, they stand it from me ! They
wince and squirm and grimace and fidget ; but they
stick it all the same. Now if I were plain ' Bill
Smith ' it'd be a different matter—the filthy snobs !
But being what I am they gasp with admiration when
I mix a few big B's in my conversation and sugar
me with their dulcet twaddle until I feel sick. Oh,
it's rare sport being cornered by some fat bediamonded
duchess, who'd hate and despise me if it mattered
a damn what she did ! I tell her what I think of
her. She smiles and shakes her head. I go one
better and give out a few oaths. She begins to gush.
I blaspheme. ˙She laughs. I become Rabelaisian.

31

She guffaws. I curse. She fawns. There is no limit to her endurance. ' For always I am Rhodes '."

While I was wondering how to reply to this amazing confession, someone came up and unhooked me.

" Rhodes," said the newcomer, " I have a special favour to ask you. Will you let me introduce you to Lady——? "

" By-bye, Codling,"said Rhodes, shaking my hand, " see you again, I suppose. You're a dirty diplomat, but I like your face."

Then, as he walked off with his friend, I heard him say : " Convey my undying hostility to Lady —— and tell her she can be introduced to me with pleasure—if she can catch me." With which words he vanished from the room and remained invisible for the rest of the afternoon. . . .

Two weeks later I find this in my diary :

" Met Rhodes at lunch to-day. He insisted on calling me ' Mr. Codling ' throughout the meal. Twice he was corrected by others, but he took no notice and went on repeating the offence. I felt rather annoyed, especially when he leant across the table during the second course and asked me in a very pointed manner whether I was enjoying the *fish*. At length I lost my temper and in answer to his question ' Oh, Mr. Codling, would you like a cod ? ' I said ' I like almost anything, Mr. Rhodes, except a cad.' The extraordinary fellow led the laughter that greeted my cheap if forgivable sally and roared out :

'Bravo! You are a man after my own heart, Codling.' . . . . "

My next sight of him was in South Africa. The moment he heard I had landed he sent a message to my hotel begging me to come and stay with him for as long as I could. I managed to put in three nights at his house, and very enjoyable they were. The "Codling" business was quite dropped and he talked on every subject that arose with the unaffected simplicity and joy of a child.

During the two days I was with him we rode about his estate and he explained everything so whole-heartedly and with such manifest pleasure that he seemed a different man from the lionized boor I had met in London. In the evenings we talked and talked —or rather he talked and I listened. An extra-ordinary fund of information he had on all sorts of topics, though his views on art were bizarre to say the least. He discussed painting as though its chief quality were the amount of canvas it covered, and literature he judged rather by output than by merit.

I had long wanted to know the truth about the Jameson Raid, and one night I cautiously approached the subject.

" I met Dr. Jameson for the first time a few weeks ago," I said. " He is a great friend of yours, isn't he ? "

Rhodes flung one leg over the arm of his chair

33

and sat gazing at me for several moments in silence. Then he said :

" Yes, you certainly ought to rise in your profession."

I laughed and asked him if he would write me a certificate.

" No," he replied promptly ; " diplomacy doesn't go down with me. I like plain thinking and plain speaking. If you ever want to get anything out of me, go straight to the point. Otherwise I shall tell you to mind your own business."

" In that case," said I, " will you please tell me to what extent you and Chamberlain were responsible for the Jameson Raid."

" That's better," he rejoined ; " now we know where we are. But you surely don't expect me to tell you, do you ? "

" Of course I don't."

" Good. Then I'll tell you."

The abruptness of his acquiescence was typical of the man.

" Naturally," he added, " if you breathe a word of what I say outside these four walls, I shall contradict all knowledge of it and call you a liar in public."

" Naturally," I affirmed.

" First of all, then," he went on, " you will believe me when I say that my evidence before the Commission was true as far as it went. The point is that it didn't go very far. That absolves me from the crime of giving false evidence on oath. The whole business, from first to last, barring a few necessary conferences in London, was hatched, outlined and arranged in this very room. Chamberlain had sounded the members of the Government. They funked an ultimatum to Kruger, said the country wouldn't stand for it. We out here knew well enough that the tide in the affairs of South Africa might at any moment turn and it was for us to take it at the flood. We also knew that even if our raid failed, it must inevitably breed bad blood and force on—war.

"Joe was with us, hand in glove. But he was quite honest about his share in the business. He told us candidly that if we failed he'd have to disown us; though by doing so he'd be able to help us. We accepted this one-sided arrangement. We had no alternative. In the muddy state of your politics there was nothing else for it. One phrase he used has always stuck in my memory. It was this : 'In a democratic state one can never fight openly for the right. In England we would have to invent an excuse to take sides with God.'

"Of course suspicion alighted on Joey; and he, being a politician, nearly let us down. If I hadn't threatened to let the cat out of the bag, the men who had helped us to win South Africa for the Empire would have served their full sentences in gaol. But I had no political axe to grind and had the power to bring Joey to heel. I held my loaded revolver at his head. 'Release *and* compensation,' I said, 'or . . . . !' He didn't like that 'or' . . . . So the

desperadoes, or patriots, or whatever you like to
call 'em—all patriots *are* desperadoes, by the way—
were released and compensated. One or two had
to be bribed to keep their mouths shut, in addition
to the 'favoured treatment' I obtained for them.
And Joey lived to fight another day ! "

This, then, for the first time is the truth of that
memorable affair, straight from the mouth of its
leading actor—or rather its stage-manager. And if
Rhodes were still alive, he'd call it a diabolical
invention from start to finish. He might even call
it by a stronger name !

§2

To leave Cecil Rhodes for Joseph Chamberlain is
exactly like leaving the wildest of backwoods for the
neatest of offices. Everything about Rhodes was
grand, primitive, disordered, and rather impossible.
Everything about Chamberlain was—well, just the
reverse. After a time one couldn't help loving
Rhodes. No one, surely, ever *loved* Chamberlain.
I certainly couldn't have done so in a hundred
years.

An excellent man to do business with—unquestionably. He knew exactly what he wanted and he knew
exactly how to get it. But out of business ? The
fact is Joey was never out of business. In his so-
called moments of recreation he thought or talked
business. No more terrible tragedy could have

overtaken him than the stroke which deprived him of his faculties for conducting business. It is just possible that the stroke made him human and lovable. I don't know, because I never spoke to him after it. But I am pretty certain that nothing short of that could have endeared him to anyone.

Strictly speaking, Chamberlain was always a figure for pity. A man who cannot relax from toil, who is lost without some work to do, is a wretched one-eyed individual. No one has worked harder at times than myself, but I should be the last to declare that work is the main object of life or that it constitutes one of its chief pleasures—even though I have greatly enjoyed some of my work. At its best work is a painful joy ; at its worst a nasty necessity. Humanity will never be half-civilized until it has learnt how to enjoy an unlimited amount of leisure time.

Chamberlain made a religion of work. When he wasn't working he was unhappy. And life took its revenge upon him by forcing him to remain inactive for his last six or seven years on earth.

I was in his company a good many times, both socially and officially, but I never knew him when his mind was not busy revolving some " scheme " to the exclusion of every other thought in the universe.

" I was made to burrow," I once heard him say.

" Yes," sighed Balfour, who was standing near, " a sort of human mole."

" Better than being a sort of languid giraffe," came

37

Joey's fierce retort—after the philosopher had moved out of earshot.

He hated Balfour, and the latter's aloof indifference to his love or loathing made him extremely bitter. This was how he described his famous colleague-antagonist in my hearing on one occasion :

" If you pricked him he'd bleed milk—sour milk."

And I cannot omit here a passage-of-arms, very characteristic of these two, which took place at a Downing Street garden-party :

B : I envy you your button-holes. Fresh from the hot-houses at Highbury, I presume ?

C : No, no. I get these in London. I seldom pick the ones at home.

B : Ah ! Fancy in flowers, practice in politics, I see.

C : One must have a fancy for something, you know —for philosophy, if everything else fails.

B : Hardly for philosophy, my dear fellow. One has to practise that.

C : Does philosophy help you in politics, then ?

B : More than in anything else.

C : How ?

B : Philosophy teaches one, for example, that man is not perfectible. If one weren't quite sure of that, no cabinet meeting would be endurable.

C : Indeed ?

B : And in word.

C : Well, if I couldn't believe in man's perfectibility, I'd blow my brains out.

B : If Campbell-Bannerman got to hear that, he'd spare no pains to make you a sceptic. But you must not confuse desire with belief.

C : I say, Balfour, I have sometimes had a horrid feeling that the perfect man, when he comes, might be something like you.

B : I, too, have been visited by that feeling, but I shouldn't describe it as horrid. In any case you need not lose your slumber over it ; because the conception, though beautiful, is, I fear, remote. A world of Balfours ! Think of it ! No, I dare not. Philosophy forbids. The Fall of Man was final. The most that can be hoped for is that he will worship the right gods.

C : Yourself, for one.

B : How admirably you read my thoughts !

C : They are too obvious to call for exceptional penetration.

B : If you will allow me to say so, my dear Chamberlain, you are becoming a trifle inharmonious.

C : Dear, dear !

B : But your orchids are divine. What an exquisite button-hole !

C : Thank you.

B : It almost makes one jealous.

C : *Could* you be jealous ?

B : Only of myself. But if anything else could make me jealous, your lovely orchids, rather than your lurid oratory, would be the cause.

C : I can think of an answer, but it's a rude one.

B : I know. Isn't it tiresome ? But I see Lady
Randolph waving to me. Have I your permission ? Thank you . . . . Some day you
must tell me the name of your florist. . . .

Here you have, in little, nearly all the salient
features of both men. Chamberlain—brusque, pre-
cise, unpolished, provocative, sincere, prosaic.
Balfour—airy, elusive, polite,irresponsible, artificial,
charmingly irritating.

To that scene I must add an encounter between
Chamberlain and myself, which dots the " i's " and
crosses the " t's " of the portrait I am trying to
paint.

At some semi-official political gathering,Chamber-
lain, in the heat of debate, had delivered himself of
several trenchant comments on the attitude of Sir
Wilfred Laurier, Prime Minister of Canada, to certain
imperial questions. These comments were excessively
indiscreet and probably quite unjust. They were,
broadly, to the effect that Laurier represented a
Catholic andNationalist minority,backed by powerful
financiers who had *bought* the Government, and whose
chief object was to throw off Canada's allegiance to
the Empire and to throw in their lot with the United
States. Laurier, therefore, as representing this faction,
was in effect a traitor, however much his present
behaviour belied it.

Needless to say this extraordinary statement was
reported by some considerate friend to Sir Wilfred,
and the incident threatened to assume imperial pro-

portions. The affair would certainly have got into the London papers if Joey hadn't used his influence. Laurier was fuming in Quebec, and already a hint of the trouble had found its way into the Canadian press.

The crisis was at its height when I arrived at headquarters after spending the better part of a year at Ottawa and Quebec. My presence was made known to Chamberlain; I was put into possession of all the facts; and, armed with a full knowledge of the feeling in Canada, I called at his office on a snowy morning in early December.

Chamberlain was talking to George Wyndham when I was shown into his sanctum. He gave me a curt nod, a " Morning," and a " Sit down."

Wyndham was looking very worried, and I noticed that he kept opening his mouth as though about to speak, then thinking better of it and shutting it again. At last Chamberlain said: " We're both getting irritable. Let's give it a rest. To-morrow at the same time. Good-bye." Then, as the door closed behind Wyndham, he turned to me with the words :

" How's Laurier ? "

This abrupt commencement to a ticklish subject took the wind clean out of my sails and I stammered : " Quite well, thank you "—or something equally inane.

" Good," said Joe ; " then it has been exaggerated. I thought so."

That brought me back with a shock to realities,

and I hastened to retrieve the position, which was getting sadly out of hand.

"I'm afraid it has not been exaggerated, Mr. Chamberlain," I said; "if anything, it has been under-stated. Sir Wilfred Laurier feels very strongly about it."

"Does he indeed? Then am I to understand that he accepts whatever trumped-up report he has received as gospel-truth?" I hesitated. "Is that so?" he rapped out.

"It has not been contradicted," I parried.

"Have I had the chance to contradict it?"

"I think so."

"How? When?"

"You might have made a guarded reference to it in the course of your last public speech, recanting what was wrong and toning down what had been exaggerated."

"When I don't even know what I'm supposed to have said?"

I didn't reply to that, because I knew he was evading the issue. He went on:

"To whom am I indebted? Who is the little bird who so thoughtfully carried my words overseas?"

"I'm afraid I——"

"Don't lie! Of course you know who it is."

"But it's hardly——"

"Yes, it is! It's of the utmost importance. Come; out with it!"

" What if I refuse ? "

" I shall refuse to—how shall we put it ?—to ease the situation."

" Will you promise to do so if I give you his name ? "

" What do you want me to do ? "

" Make a personal explanation to Laurier, contradict the report he received—and perhaps refer to him eulogistically in some future speech."

" But what if I mean every word I said—and more ? "

" As a Minister of the Crown you couldn't mean it."

" No ? Very well. I'll apologize for the Minister of the Crown."

At that I gave him the name he wanted. It caused him no little amazement.

" You're very trusting," he observed, reverting to our agreement ; " suppose I now go back on my word ? "

" You won't," I replied with conviction.

" Why ? "

" Because you are a gentleman."

" Wrong ! " he cried with a chuckle. " I'm not a gentleman. I wouldn't be where I am if I had been a gentleman. No gentleman ever fights the world and beats it with its own weapons. Now Balfour's a gentleman. He can afford to be. But I'll keep my word. Would you like to know why ? "

" Very much."

" Because a bargain's a bargain, and I'm a man of business. Good-morning."

He got up briskly, shook my hand, waved to the door, and was busy with the papers on his desk before I had left the room.

CHAPTER IV

THE PEACEMAKER

King Edward VII

EASILY the most interesting and versatile personality among the reigning monarchs of my time was King Edward VII. I came into contact with him so often that my diary literally teems with anecdotes, from which it is difficult to make a selection. However, I will do the best I can and leave my readers to form their own conclusions as to his character and attainments. Having no desire to act as special pleader on behalf of anyone, I permit my subjects to sketch themselves whenever possible, withholding nothing of importance and nothing that will help to make the portraits as many-sided as possible.

Edward VII was, though few people realized it, a man of moods. He had, for instance, a " practical joke " mood and a *lèse majesté* mood ; and a fellow who had known him only as a practical joker might at any moment run his head against the stone wall of His Majesty's dignity and suffer a terrible eclipse. I knew a case of this sort.

THE WHISPERING GALLERY

A certain Frenchman, still alive, used to amuse
King Edward during many of the monarch's leisure
hours at Biarritz. He was quick-witted and full of
fun and invention. Incidentally he was a bit of a
conjurer, and used to entertain the King at all sorts
of odd moments by producing the most absurd objects
from the most impossible places. One day he was
at the top of his form and contrived to spirit a
tortoise into a despatch-box belonging to the King—
at least he certainly produced it from there, so I
assumed he had had previous access to the box.
Edward, who had been roaring with laughter at
such feats as the wholesale production of balls and
matches from everybody's beard or pocket, suddenly
became grave and addressed the conjurer as follows :

"I must ask for an explanation of that trick."

The Frenchman—not sensing the change in the
wind, having had no previous experience of hostile
gusts—cried out that he would be enchanted to clear
up the mystery and promptly brought forth another
tortoise from another despatch-box.

His Majesty was really angry now and said :

"There are papers in those boxes of great importance——"

But the Frenchman was too excited to notice the
lowering sky and chipped in :

"Then you'll have to appoint the tortoises to
your Privy Council to keep them quiet. I promise
they'll be no slower than the majority of Privy
Councillors!"

So far they had both spoken in French; but now the King came out with a few crisp English phrases. They sounded strangely harsh in comparison, and as he spoke them in his most guttural manner the conjurer tumbled quickly to their intent:

"Understand, sir, I am not joking. This is serious. Were those tortoises in those boxes?"

For answer the Frenchman walked up to the boxes and tried to open them. They were locked securely.

"But how——?" began His Majesty. "I mean I saw you open them."

The Frenchman deftly lifted one of the boxes, making a pass over it with his other hand as he did so, and the movement certainly gave one the impression that the lid was being opened.

"I beg your pardon," said the King gruffly. Then, turning on his heel, he left the room.

But he was enjoying the society of the *prestidigitateur* the following day with as much relish as ever. . . .

His generosity and kindness of heart were remarkable, and the best instance of this that I remember occurred when he was Prince of Wales.

One day in the later nineties I was driving with him and two other friends through the streets of Cannes. He was not being recognized and was enjoying the drive as a consequence. Suddenly he leant across and spoke to one of his friends, a French Count of great social brilliance and some literary distinction, who was sitting by my side and facing him :

" Tell me : who is that stout fellow dawdling by the kiosk over there ? "

" That is an Englishman, or rather Irishman, your Royal Highness."

" I thought so. And his name ? "

" Oscar Wilde."

" Good God ! " said the Prince and leant back in his seat.

The rest of us looked with great curiosity at the man who, a few years before, had lorded it over society and was now an outcast. The Prince noticed our interest and begged us not to " cut " him if he caught us gazing at him. Instantly we all faced about and looked in another direction. Our action was not lost on the Prince, who leant right out of the carriage, caught Wilde's eye, and removed his hat.

Wilde was either too absorbed or too amazed to return the salute. It may have seemed to him too much like a dream of the past to be true. Whatever the cause, he stood stock-still on the *pavé*, staring apathetically after the retreating vehicle.

" Poor devil ! " sighed the Prince—and again " Poor devil ! " Later I heard him say, obviously in pursuance of a train of thought, " What can one do ? " Later still I heard him inquire of his friend, the French Count, whether it would be possible to get into touch with Wilde without giving the tongue of scandal a chance to wag. I am quite certain that, if he found a way of helping the poet, he did not fail to do so.

To that episode I might add, merely as a matter of social history, that I once heard the Prince describe Wilde as " the most charming personality of the age "—and he had certainly met the pick of personalities. . . .

" One of the saddest things in life," he once said to me, " is that nearly every man is cut off, by differences in outlook and temperament, from his parents and children. I was as fond of my father as he allowed me to be. We didn't understand one another. My mother, whom I greatly admired, hated me, because she imagined that I had hastened my father's death. I never in my life had a real heart-to-heart talk with her. Whenever we were together, either she was upbraiding me or I was chafing under her total inability to understand me and her refusal to trust me, which of course she construed into a fit of the sulks. Towards the end of her life we were mutually obnoxious, and I never left her presence without a sigh of relief.

" As to my own children," he went on, " I had nothing in common with my eldest son, and I have very little in common with my second. Since he has been heir to the throne we have drifted still further apart. He doesn't care for my friends, and I don't care for his. He isn't interested in my pursuits and I'm not interested in his. We both enjoy a good dinner, but there our common tastes both start and finish. Every effort I make to get into closer touch and sympathy with him seems to end in our becoming more and more estranged. It's heart-breaking—this antagonism between different generations. One can neither bridge the chasm between the present and the past nor span the abyss between the present and the future. Perhaps we are not meant to."

He seldom gave way to such melancholy reflections; yet it would be wrong to paint him without suggesting those shadows.

King Edward was at his greatest as a diplomat, but before I depict him in that rôle—surely the best that can become a monarch—I would like to illustrate the shrewdness of his judgment on contemporary men and affairs. I therefore take some of his sayings at random from my diary.

Asked one day why he never read books, he replied :

" For precisely the same reason that I never *taste* wine. You can get about as much life in a book as you can get wine in a sip. I like life as I like wine —in full measure and running over."

Someone wanted his opinion of Mark Twain, whom he had just met. This was his comment :

" A great teller of stories, the padding of which is more important than the point. One story he told me was developing at such alarming length and in such detail that I begged him to cut it short and come to the point. He replied: 'There is no point,' and left the full story untold—to my unspeakable relief. He seems to hover on the verge of saying something. But he never says it."

Of his biographer, Sir Sidney Lee, he said:

" He deserves the thanks of all Englishmen for making out Shakespeare to have been true to the national type—that is, a model of respectability and business acumen. I am quite positive our national poet was nothing of the sort—so our gratitude to his biographer is doubled ! "

Of Disraeli he said:

" The only indisputable humbug who was also a great man. Personally I couldn't stand him ; but I could never ask for a greater Prime Minister, and I would never see one half as great."

Of Gladstone he said:

" A shocking Prime Minister, but a wonderful fellow. People say he was a humbug. Rubbish ! If he had been, he'd have imposed on my mother, who, being very simple, could never see through humbugs, and consequently adored them. But Gladstone missed his true vocation. He was a born schoolmaster. The only times I ever enjoyed learning anything were the odd hours I spent in his company. His knowledge was unrivalled and seemed almost unlimited, but he never pumped it into you. He realized to a nicety how much you could stand and never gave you a drop too much. And as he suited his method to his audience he never bored anyone.

For ' learning without tears ' commend me to Gladstone. He should have taught the nation—but from the class-room not from Westminster."

The Irish question worried him a lot from time to time. This was how he once disposed of it in my hearing :

" For God's sake let them have Home Rule ! Then *we'll* have Home Rule "—meaning the disappearance of the Irish Party from Westminster.

The Tariff Reform controversy amused him. He never discussed it seriously, though I recall one phrase he let drop :

" A healthy country needs no tariff, and no tariffs can save an unhealthy country. These drugs are useless."

He was not much given to prophecy, but I cannot help making public the following :

" Monarchical government in England is popular only in proportion as the monarch is popular. It is the man who counts, not the institution. The world is being inoculated so thoroughly nowadays with anti-monarchical ideas that, unless he can do something that will appeal strongly to the popular imagination, I doubt if the Kingship will survive my grandson."

As I have said, it was as a diplomat, as a master of my own profession, that King Edward shone with peculiar refulgence ; and it so happens that I can show him at work on one of the most ticklish jobs he ever had to handle. The scene which I am about to describe also paints the other leading character (Kaiser Wilhelm) to the life. It took place during the German Emperor's last visit to England, in the presence of myself and a German Count, as representing our respective Services.

It was supposed to be a purely formal talk, in which the general tendencies of European policy would be glanced at and an understanding reached between the greatest military and the greatest naval power in the world. The two protagonists disliked one another—of that there can be no doubt. The history of their mutual antipathy is too long and complicated to go into. Nor does it concern my purpose here. The fact remains that, mentally and temperamentally, they were utterly incompatible. For the rest, their characters will appear in what follows in the strongest possible contrast.

After a few pleasant trivialities in connection with his luncheon with the Lord Mayor of London the previous day, Wilhelm said:

"I was never so struck by anything as the sturdiness of the types I meet in England wherever I go. So unlike the Latin folk. Real blood-brothers we are, eh?"

Edward nodded his head and murmured something about "cousins-german" and "German cousins." The Kaiser continued:

"Between us we could conquer the world—I mean we could keep the peace of the world."

A short pause ; then the duologue began :

ED :   There is already a balance of power.

WM :   Yes, but we could change it.

ED :   Break word, you mean.

WM :   No, no. Cancel a contract by mutual agreement.

ED :   Would it, in every case, be mutual ?

WM :   What does that matter ? It's not a case for individual taste but for international betterment.

ED :   I see. Well, what is your suggestion ?

WM :   First of all I take it I am rightly informed over your Entente with France ? (*Edward doesn't answer.*) It's only an excuse to make noises at one another across the Channel ?

ED :   (*smiling*) That's it.

WM :   Good. Then it needn't detain us. France wouldn't dare to move without your consent, because you could blockade her on the north, the west and the south. That merely leaves Russia—your ancient antagonist and ours——

ED :   Not so fast. You haven't yet told me why you want to change the balance of power.

WM :   (*striking the table*) To keep the peace of the world.

ED :   Is that the only reason ?

WM :   Certainly.

ED :   What about parcelling out some of the territories owned by France in Africa ?

WM :   Yes, there's something in that.

ED :   And taking Alsace-Lorraine off her hands?

WM :   (*catching fire*) Excellent!

ED :   And sharing between us the entire Mahommedan world?

WM :   (*exultantly*) You paint my dreams!

ED :   Possibly; but I wonder whether the world will remain at peace while we are doing all these things.

WM :   What does that matter? Between us we can silence the rest of the world.

ED :   After that you could silence us?

WM :   Eh? My dear uncle, what do you mean?

ED :   You have forgotten Italy and Turkey.

WM :   I can't trust Italy. With you in the Mediterranean, she'd never dare fight us.

ED :   I'm glad to hear that.

WM :   (*flurried*) You don't understand me. You're trying to trip me up.

ED :   Please don't say that. I'm trying to get a clear perspective. How does Turkey stand?

WM :   (*suddenly cautious and sullen*) I don't know.

ED :   But you must have an inkling.

WM :   (*firing up*) You don't imagine, do you, that I'm going to show you all my cards and let you keep yours up your sleeve?

ED :   You have only to say the word and I'll produce them for your inspection.

WM :   (*brightening*) Then what engagements have you got with other countries?

ED :   Military? None.

WM : You really mean that if there was a war in Europe to-morrow, you'd have to look for your allies ?

ED : I do.

WM : Gott in Himmel !

ED : But I want peace. One does not require military allies to ensure peace.

WM : Ha ! That's stupid ! That's ridiculous ! In these affairs, uncle, you are a child.

ED : Perhaps.

WM : But of course ! I tell you it's foolish. We are your natural allies.

ED : You say Turkey would like ￲to kick us out of the East.

WM : Naturally. (*His countryman plucks at his sleeve.*) I beg your pardon. I said nothing of the sort.

ED : Well, you intimated——

WM : (*bursting in*) Turkey's aspirations are amusing. We wouldn't let her do anything we didn't wish her to do.

ED : Certainly we would take a lot of beating. But, having settled Europe between us, what would our next object be ?

WM : (*excitedly*) America !

ED : What should we want with America ?

WM : Germanize it—that is, Teutonize it.

ED : That's a weightier proposition altogether.

WM : (*cunningly*) Worthy of the Anglo-Saxon race.

ED : Yes.

WM : (*enthusiastically*) You think so ?

ED : Undoubtedly.

WM : Then it's agreed?

ED : I will speak to my ministers.

WM : You will try to persuade them?

ED : I will put the whole matter before them.

WM : It would be a great thing for England.

ED : And for Germany.

WM : *Ach*, we Germans think of the world.

ED : I know you do.

In a remarkably short space of time the Kaiser had managed to tell Edward everything the latter wanted to know, partly led on by his own impetuousness and partly entrapped by the King of England's superior intelligence. Wilhelm never thoroughly realized that Edward was egging him on, though clearly a suspicion crossed his mind at one moment that Edward was not quite such a fool as he made himself out to be.

In the same space of time Edward had contrived to tell Wilhelm literally nothing, though he had done it without any excess of caution, leaving the Kaiser completely unsuspicious that he had aroused any of his uncle's suspicions.

The talk then centred on a topic that eventually formed the subject of a Foreign Office despatch, and ended up with several playful and facetious comments by the German Emperor on Bulwer Lytton's " Money," which he had seen a night or two before at a Command Performance at Drury Lane Theatre.

CHAPTER V

THREE CÆSARS

Kaiser Wilhelm II, Tsar Nicholas II, Emperor Francis Joseph.

§I

I REALIZE that in withholding my name I am running the risk of not being believed. All these conversations between famous folk, which I have reproduced as correctly as mortal could, will probably sound strange to that vast outside world that knows nothing of our notabilities except what it reads of them in ill-informed gossip columns and unauthentic memoirs. Surely, I can hear some of my readers saying, the Kaiser couldn't have been such a fool as this man paints him. Surely these celebrities weren't quite as silly and commonplace as he makes them out to be.

Well, I can only tell you that thirty years in the diplomatic service and a more than nodding acquaintance with these makers of history have convinced me that the majority of self-made famous men achieved their eminence by virtue of their excessive ordinariness, by the extremity and intensity of their reactions to the commonest impulses ; and that the rest of them, those who were born eminent, attained whatever popularity they possessed by their defects rather than their finer qualities.

Let me admit that I have only met three truly great men in my life. Two of them were utterly unknown and the third was never regarded as such. As to the remainder, I must ask you to take my word that the portraits in this book *are* portraits, and not caricatures ; and that, though I do not claim for them absolute verisimilitude (for who but God can see the whole of a man ?), I do know them to be perfectly faithful representations of certain aspects which have been revealed to me.

I would like now to give miniatures, so to speak, of the three Cæsars who ruled the greater part of Europe before the 1914—18 war put an end to their dynasties and activities. First, both in importance and interest, there was the Kaiser.

Wilhelm was a man of untiring vitality and super-ficial versatility. On the whole, in my personal dealings with him, I liked him—chiefly perhaps because he really did put all his cards on the table. The one thing that he was accused of throughout the war was the one thing every single person who had ever met him *knew* to be false. He was not and never could be a Machiavelli. To put it bluntly, he was too much of a fool to be one. The dis-tinguishing feature of his character was its childish (I had almost said its babyish) simplicity. He blurted things out in a manner that caused his discreet ministers perpetual, harassing, hair-whitening anxiety. He was known among us, unofficially, as " the school-boy." He couldn't be trusted with a secret, and the chief job of his Chancellor was to keep him from suspecting the existence of a State agreement or Treaty before it was framed and accepted by the contracting parties.

Von Bülow, who was the essence of discretion, once said to a colleague of mine : " Thank God no one outside Germany takes him seriously ! "

The Kaiser was all surface. He had no discover-able depths. He loved dressing-up and all the paraphernalia of ceremony. He loved his pet regi-ments, just as a child loves its favourite box of soldiers ; and when he reviewed one of them after the battles round Verdun, he wept—not, I am sure, because so many had been killed, but because their usually smart uniforms had been soiled.

Everyone in this country imagines he was devoted to his grandmother, Queen Victoria. On the con-trary, he hated her for reading him so many lectures, and once in a fit of spoilt-boy passion he cried out : " She'll be sorry for that one day ! " And on another occasion : " Her silly sermons are wasted on me, but I shall teach her a lesson she won't forget." Which of course proved that one of her " silly sermons," though wasted no doubt, had at least gone home.

Yes, he was unquestionably a simpleton, but not

intentionally a guileless one. He harboured designs against peoples and countries, but he couldn't help telling them all about it and putting them on the alert. There was not a single responsible minister of the English Crown who was not quite well aware that the Kaiser had publicly threatened us with castigation in the year 1911 (a minute made by myself placed the information before the Cabinet), but they pooh-poohed it as another of his " absurd antics." It certainly was another of his antics. But the peculiar nature of its absurdity was brought home to us three years later.

Mostly, of course, my meetings with Wilhelm were at State functions, but twice I had private interviews with him at Potsdam. At the first of these he was in one of his light-hearted humorous moods and tried to prove that Shakespeare was a German, the chief evidence that he could bring being that no German is introduced into any of the plays ! When I informed him that the same sort of evidence proved conclusively that Homer was an Englishman, he laughed and said : " You can have him ! It doesn't much matter."

Then he said :

" Who is this man Shaw some of my people are getting so interested in ? Tell me about him."

" He's a very clever Irishman," I replied, " who finds that the English people will actually pay him for poking fun at them."

" What a strange race you are ! " he exclaimed.

" I don't think we would pay anyone to do that. But tell me more. Is he *really* clever, or just funny? Is he as clever as I am? "

" As clever as you are? " I echoed.

" Yes. Could he govern Germany? " pursued Wilhelm.

" I've no doubt he'd like to," I said, rather at a loss for an answer.

" But could he?—could he?—could he? " the Kaiser shouted.

" He'd write an admirable preface on how it ought to be governed," said I ; " but I'm sure he wouldn't govern it like you."

That seemed to satisfy him, because he laughed with unnecessary vehemence for about half a minute before saying :

" Oh, these dreamers and talkers ! Where would the world be without its doers? My son says he is merely another of the many dangerous fools about. You are a queer mixture, with your Irishmen and Shakespeares and Jews all rubbing each other's shoulders. Lucky for you that you had Lord Beaconsfield. His politics did more for you than the poetry of the others."

He was in high spirits that day—quite a different man from the serious monarch whom I spoke with on my second visit to Potsdam.

This second visit occurred at a time when a fearful scandal had just shaken the German Court from its head downwards, and public exposures of a terrifying nature were threatened. The Kaiser had retired to Potsdam in a fit of depression, and I heard that I was the first person he had seen for more than a week who was neither a minister nor a friend.

Knowing that the subject was in everyone's mouth, he made no attempt to conceal his chagrin from me, and before I had been in his company for five minutes he burst out with the following:

"It is incredible that I should have to put up with this sort of thing! As if my other responsibilities were not sufficiently worrying! What will they say in France and England? I shall be the butt of Europe. It's intolerable, preposterous, *schrecklich!* How dare they rake up all this filth? It's bad enough to *know* it, but to have it known is unbearable. And what's the good? Tell me that. What's the good? *Es ist schmutzig!*"

The amount of guttural repulsion he got into this last word made me realize, not for the first time, that he was a born actor. For several minutes he walked up and down the room, hitting his chest at intervals with one of his fists, and making throaty ejaculations. Then he tired of it, sat down very suddenly bolt upright in a swivel-chair, and turned to other topics, twisting himself alternately towards me and away from me as he emphasized his points:

"Where would you be if I didn't keep the peace of Central Europe?" he asked.

"Well——" I began; but he wasn't interested in my hesitations.

" I will tell you. Between the devil of France and the deep sea of the Mahommedan world. Don't imagine that France loves you. She doesn't. She hates you. She's jealous of you. She'll never forgive you for all her defeats. Think of them—Egypt, Canada, India. She had her footing in all of them and you have pushed her out. Don't be deceived. She'll make love to you ; she's doing it now ; but in her heart there is hatred and jealousy. Suppose you fought with her against me. Fools ! Can't you see that that's what she wants ? Suppose you helped her against me ? Suppose you got Russia to back you ? Suppose you won ? You wouldn't, but suppose you did ? What then ? What sort of an alliance would you be likely to make with a natural and hereditary enemy like her ? Pfff ! The future lies with the Teutonic peoples. Your future lies with ours, ours with yours. The Latin civiliza-tion is effete, second-rate, out-of-date. We Teutons must finish the work. Do you hear ? I am telling you what to expect if you choose France instead of Germany. You will ally yourselves with the past and turn your backs upon the rising sun. Remember what I say."

" But——" I began again. He brushed my thoughts aside and went on :

" Listen ! France would never forgive you if you helped to save her. It would increase her load of envy. She'd plot and plot and plot. Already she has begun to undermine your Empire. Do you know what she is doing in Morocco? She is fraternizing with the Mahommedan world. She will sap your strength in the East. I know. I *know*. That is her game. You do not believe me? Well, you will see. I am not blind. I tell you I know."

He spoke throughout in a sharp, staccato manner, and once or twice I noticed that his mouth twitched with the effort of keeping control over his voice. There was passion and excitement behind his words which belied the studied statuesqueness of his physical pose.

At this point I managed to get in a phrase before he recommenced his vocal operations:

"France is no fonder of Germany than she is of England," I said.

Instead of treating me to another deluge of words, he looked at me in silence for a few moments before saying:

"You really think so?"

I answered that I did.

"Sedan is further off than Suez," he replied.

Then he jumped up and our conversation was at an end. . . .

§2

My second Cæsar was in startling contrast to his German rival. The Tsar of all the Russias was subtle, not simple, but his subtlety was barbaric while the Kaiser's simplicity was comparatively

65

civilized. In effect this means that Wilhelm was the sort of boy who puts out his tongue in public, whereas Nicholas was the sort of boy who pulls off the legs of flies in private.

Both children, both half-finished products, both in the long run harmful. But individually quite different. There was nothing fundamentally sinister in the soul of Wilhelm. He was a well-meaning fool. But the soul of Nicholas was a horrible, distorted thing. He was an ill-meaning skunk.

I am not saying this because I personally disliked Nicholas. Some of the most delightful people I have ever met have been among the biggest scoundrels of their time. I neither liked him nor disliked him. I am simply speaking of what I know to have been true. However, I am in a position to substantiate my view with several instances of his primitive proclivities.

One day a pamphlet by a student of Odessa got into the hands of the police. It happened to contain an attack on the Romanoff régime, with a reference to its diseased stock as exemplified by the physical condition of the Tsar's little son.

Nicholas was told of this pamphlet and insisted upon seeing it. The reference to his child made him livid with fury. He ordered the student to be brought before him. The unfortunate pamphleteer, trussed like a fowl for roasting, was carried into his presence ; and Nicholas—" Little Father " of his people, high and mighty monarch of all the Russias

—glutted his sadist rage by having the youth thrashed with a whip until he fainted.

Though his behaviour proved the student's contention up to the hilt, the latter died in Siberia for daring to suggest that the stock of the Romanoffs was degenerate!

Nicholas went in terror of his life. He believed every cock-and-bull story of attempted assassination that came his way. In such a manner did his "favourites" and relations prey upon his unhinged imagination.

Once he was told about a small political club which met subterraneously and plotted the overthrow of his dynasty. Actually the club was composed of the sworn enemies of two of his pet advisers. Without going into the matter at all carefully, but acting under the influence of panic, he gave orders for the members to be arrested, tried and shot before midnight. Such a thing as mercy was foreign to his diseased temperament. His was the true coward's motto : when in doubt, KILL! Without any hope of appeal and without the least consciousness of crime those men were solemnly butchered. Their heinous offence had lain solely in their courageous hatred of the lickspittle pimps who surrounded the Russian Emperor.

I am told, in the common phraseology of our Christian era, that Nicholas expiated his faults in the manner of his own death. But I do not accept that particular kind of sentimental balderdash. No man ever *expiates* his faults. All that he can plead in his favour (if he's lucky) is an equal number of virtues. We cannot undo what we have done. We can only not go on doing it. The man who believes that one good act can atone for one bad act is a fool, and the man who lives on such an assumption is a coward. Official Christianity thrives on that kind of caddish blackguardism ; but the better Christians know better.

Nicholas was a cad, a coward, a butcher and a blackguard. If any man ever deserved his fate, he certainly did ; and if the Bolshevik revolution had been infinitely worse than even the English press painted it, anyone who knew the Romanoffs must be forever astounded at the moderation of the revolutionaries. But if Nicholas had been murdered in cold blood a thousand times over, it would not have balanced the account—even on the silly principle of " a life for a life."

I could give countless instances of his detestable cruelty, but that has already been done by many men who witnessed it at first-hand. Equally I could give innumerable examples of his snivelling sentimentality—I have observed that bullies and cowards are nearly always sentimentalists—but one will suffice.

During the war a close friend of his was shot, and not long afterwards died. The Tsar was frantic in his sorrow, wept, tore his hair and raved in his prayers to God. No doubt to soothe his aching heart the Almighty managed to convey, per special messenger, the stirring information that his friend had been shot in the back—foully.

The " Little Father " proceeded personally to the scene of slaughter and added to the number of dead recumbent upon the ground a further six—the complete private bodyguard of his much-loved friend. I should add that, as far as could be ascertained, none of the six had been remotely responsible for the demise of the dear departed.

The Great Emperor then returned to his headquarters, much gratified and even elevated by the retaliatory measures he had taken, his faith in the goodness of God unshaken, and firm in the belief that his friend's soul would rest more securely in peace on account of the welcome presence of the six souls of his private bodyguard to keep him company —or perhaps to guard his soul in heaven more efficiently than they had guarded his body on earth !

It is now my duty to tell the truth about the diplomatic exchanges between the Tsar and the Kaiser at a time when France was assured of the help of Russia in the event of war with Germany. Certainly not more than half a dozen people ever saw that correspondence. The Tsar's originals and copies of Wilhelm's replies were either destroyed, hidden, or carried away by the Kaiser when he went to Holland. What happened to the Tsar's copies and Wilhelm's originals I do not know.

The letters evidently commenced shortly after one or two preliminary conversations. They assumed throughout a basis of discussion which had obviously been agreed upon earlier. I mean that the monarchs had clearly determined it was in their interests to make an alliance if only they could arrange mutually satisfactory terms.

The Tsar's first letter (I speak from notes made at the time, 1910) explained briefly the nature of his alliance with France. But he remarked that it was absurd to expect a modern democracy like France to have any sympathy with or understanding of his government. Russia had far more in common with Germany, he hinted, than either could ever have with France.

The Kaiser's reply was guarded but hopeful. He said that it was his dearest wish to form an alliance with his great eastern neighbour, but that it would take time to accustom his people to the idea and it would be necessary to give them sound guarantees of goodwill. What did Nicholas suggest?

Nicholas suggested, in letter number two, that Constantinople should be handed over to Russia.

Wilhelm replied (1) that such an arrangement could hardly be described as a gesture of goodwill on the part of Russia towards Germany, and (2) that as he had a personal understanding with the present occupants of Constantinople, he would rather like to consult them before presenting it to another country.

The Tsar, in letter number three, explained at great length why the occupation of Constantinople by Russia would greatly benefit Germany. The reasons he gave were various and curious. For example, he contended that Germany would have an outlet to the Black Sea via the Balkans and a further outlet to the Mediterranean Sea via the Dardanelles. Together, he urged, they could check England's eastern activities.

The Kaiser's reply was that he was already checking England's eastern activities with the assistance of Turkey, and he asked the Tsar if he could suggest any basis of agreement which did not include the Russianization of Constantinople.

Nicholas answered (letter number four) that he would give Wilhelm *carte blanche* in the Balkans in exchange for his insistence on the evacuation of Constantinople by Turkey.

The Kaiser asked where the Turks were to go?

Nicholas suggested Jerusalem. That, he remarked naively, would solve all difficulties.

Here there was a lapse of several weeks; after which, in his reply to the Tsar's fifth letter, the German Emperor stated quite flatly that the evacuation of Constantinople by Turkey could not be discussed. It was not practical politics.

Nicholas countered this, in a sixth letter, with something that almost amounted to a threat. He very nearly said that the Hohenzollern dynasty would stand or fall on the Kaiser's decision with regard to Constantinople. But, as a last throw, he concluded with a promise to allow Germany to annex France in return for the Kaiser's compliance with his near-eastern project.

The representative of the Hohenzollern dynasty was too ruffled by the threat to pay much attention to the promise. He roundly informed the heir of the Romanoffs that Constantinople would only be taken by Russia over his dead body, that the Turks were his friends and allies, and that, when the time came to annex France, he would not ask the permission of Nicholas before doing so.

Altogether an amusing and instructive correspondence, my brief record being quite sufficient to prove that the war was not wholly fought in vain if its only tangible result was the removal of these two gentlemen from their sphere of activities. . . .

§3

In comparison with the Kaiser and the Tsar, the third Cæsar in pre-war Europe was humdrum ; which means of course that he was a safer monarch than either of the others. When I knew him Francis Joseph was a tired old man with a penchant for smutty stories. The twin-diadem of Austria and Hungary sat heavily upon that wrinkled brow and he turned with relief to the coruscations of the pornographers.

Once I was taken into his confidence and to this day I can see the old fellow leaning over the arm of his chair and wheezing his disillusions asthmatically into my left ear :

"I have had enough of it all," he said, speaking in stilted French. "I have tasted greatness and it has turned to ashes in my mouth. The best people I have met in my life have been the common people. Isn't that a curious confession? But it is true, nevertheless. Only think of the others—the lords and ladies, their satellites and underlings. What of truth and common honesty is there in all this miserable round of so-called social life? I have yet to find it. Time-servers, place-finders—all of them. I have seen through them—yes, truly—and in the solitary places of my soul I have laughed—laughed to see them bow and scrape, laughed to see their fear, laughed at them in the height of their fame, laughed at them in the depth of their infamy. They are a pack of little fools, sycophants, exposing their emptiness and silliness to the ringing laughter of their own tin gods . . . . I'm weary of it all, weary even of my own cousin-kings and princes. . . . There's a shady lot for you! Little Napoleon—that comical upstart who tried to make me look foolish—was a gentleman compared with most of the others. . . .

"This is the day of democracy. Well, I'll tell you a thing or two. The only power that ever kept the world civilized and sane is this same autocracy which I am supposed to represent and which is going a little out of fashion. Autocracy means discipline, order, reason. You smile? Yet consider. There can be no discipline, order, reason, from a mob. There can be only anarchy. Nature itself is the servant of one inexorable law. Can Man defy the law of Nature ? Religion is autocratic, what you call Evolution is mercilessly autocratic, God is autocratic or He is not God. Therefore I say that man's natural government is an autocracy. And you will find throughout history that, just as at every emotional crisis man has turned to God, so also at every physical crisis man has turned to autocratic government. As surely as he cries for a God does he cry for a Man. This is true. I know it. . . .

" But it is hard on the autocrat. He must bend his back to the slavery of command—the worst of all slaveries, because it must be endured alone. Doesn't your national poet say ' Uneasy lies the head that wears a crown ' ? How true ! . . . . Ah, that reminds me of a story. . . ."

It reminded him of an unprintable story of a broadly obstetrical nature. Indeed we passed the next half-hour in (for my part) pseudo-jocular appreciation of a series of Decameronic incidents. His own affection for this species of entertainment was made audible at times by a number of sounds that reminded me of nothing so much as the distant whinnying of a horse.

Suddenly he stopped short in the middle of a yarn that threatened to overstep the limits of regal decorum and said :

" Think of an orgy of killing ! Nero had the idea. Old men become tired of everything except the sight of blood. A gory spectacle—yes, that might arouse even a centenarian, that should satiate the otherwise unappeasable cravings of senility. Horrible, horrible!" (He shuddered.) "But beautiful to jaded appetites, eh?" (He whinnied.) "Have you ever heard of Francisco de Carbajal?"

I replied that the portrait of that gentleman was one of the most memorable things in a book that was the admiration of the English-speaking world.

"Naturally," said he, "naturally." (Another whinny.) "How stupid of me! Prescott has immortalized the dear fellow. Now I will tell you a story about Francisco which will be new to you. . . ."

I'm afraid that story, too, is hardly fit for publication in this Puritanical age. But the way in which the old Emperor gloated over its telling made me profoundly thankful that it was not my duty to wait upon him daily. There was something a trifle creepy about this particular aspect of his dotage.

To be honest, however, I must admit that there was a great deal of natural charm about the last of the reigning Hapsburgs. In spite of the fact that, according to his confession, he despised the lords and ladies of his Court, he was at his very best during big State occasions, and I doubt if any monarch of his time could laugh and joke so familiarly without losing a jot of dignity. He always had the right word for everybody, from a servant to an Archduke, and he was the only one of my three Cæsars who had any real sympathy with the common people he governed or the least understanding of their needs.

CHAPTER VI

TWO DESPOTS

Lenin, Mussolini.

§1

I CANNOT do better than follow my chapter on the three pre-war Cæsars with portraits of the two post-war Dictators. But as the primary object of this book is to get at the truth and tell it, I must be honest with my readers throughout and let them know when I am not speaking from first-hand knowledge.

What follows, then, is a " likeness " of Vladimir Ilyich Lenin, whom I never met, drawn from conversations with several friends who did meet him and carefully entered in my diary at the time of their occurrence. In this case, therefore, you are receiving at second-hand what I received at first-hand.

Of course Lenin was a fanatic ; but not in the old-fashioned meaning of the word. For though oppression kindled the fire of fanaticism in him, education and art gave him flexibility. He was that modern paradox : a flexible fanatic. In practice this meant that though his life was guided and governed by the vision of an Utopia, he was quite willing to adopt any reasonable expedient to bring it about. Most emphatically the one thing he could not be called was the one thing Mr. H. G. Wells called him—the Dreamer of the Kremlin. On several occasions he had the unprecedented courage to proclaim his errors and publicly recant. Indeed he would have been quite willing to alter every item in his programme—except the Grand Finale.

There was about him an impersonal kindness, a concrete coldness but an abstract warmth. One half of him was pure brute, the other half demi-god. There was hardly any room in his strangely complex personality for what is known as common humanity. His actions were never the effect of sentiment but of sense.

His ordinary conversation was crisp, direct and frankly indiscreet. He did not, like the vast majority of politicians, commence an answer to a plain question by giving a history of the difficulties against which he had to contend ; nor did he ever fall back upon his underlings to help him out of a hole. When he was in a hole he was perfectly willing to inform anybody of the fact and openly discuss the ways and means of getting out of it. He absolutely rejected the methods of mystification so popular with other statesmen and left one under no illusion as to his real opinions on every subject he discussed.

He hated private quarrels and bickerings, because the time and energy devoted to them were lost to the State. Above all he had a keen sense of humour. This kept him sane when everyone about him was in a condition that could only be described as pathological. His eyes were smiling and kindly. They suggested success in the boudoir rather than the bureau. But the mouth belied them. It was firm and powerful. The eyes attracted one in his presence. The mouth remained in the memory. Three or four stories, all of them substantiated by my friends, will round off the picture I have given.

Shortly after he came to power it got about that he was offering the Germans an unconditional peace. The news brought forth a mob of so-called patriots, who paraded the streets with banners and shouted for a continuance of the war. Lenin sent for the ringleaders and wanted to know their grievance They asked him what he intended to do in regard to the war.

" Beg the Germans to make peace," he replied.

" On dishonourable terms ? " they questioned.

" No terms are dishonourable," he answered ; " the moment you make terms they become honourable ; you only call them dishonourable if you don't want to make them. It is not worth our while fighting Germany, so I shall stop the war. We have quite enough to do to attend to our own troubles."

" But what if they refuse to stop it unless we surrender the country ? " he was asked.

" They are quite welcome to the country if they care to take it," replied Lenin ; " I certainly shan't stop them. We can go on retreating and retreating before their victorious armies until we are behind the Urals. If they care to follow us still further, there is quite a respectable stretch of country between that and Kam chatka. From their point of view the only drawback to such a campaign would be the very tiresome walk home at its conclusion."

The patriots were not quite certain whether "Father Lenin" was serious or pulling their legs, and one of their number went so far as to say that death was better than surrender.

"Oh, I see what vexes you now!" exclaimed the Dictator—"You really want to die in the trenches. How silly of me not to have thought of that before! Of course you shall, my brothers. Believe me, I should be the last to stand in your way . . . . I give you full permission to go as soon as you like and embrace the death of heroes. You may even, if you wish, go as far as Berlin and dictate your own terms of peace."

"Then you will help us?" came in faltering tones from one of the whilom diehards.

"To the very best of my ability," returned Lenin promptly—"only"—he rubbed his chin in some perplexity—"I shan't be able to give you any boots for several months, and I regret to say there aren't any overcoats available for the winter that is almost upon us. However, such obstacles are not insuperable to men of your courage and capability; for you can take enough boots from the Germans you kill and you will doubtless have finished the war before the snow begins to fall. Everything else you shall certainly have, except—dear me! how thoughtless of me to forget it!—except ammunition. You see, our supplies from England have been entirely cut off, and—but, my dear friends, what is worrying you now?"

His dear friends were leaving the room in an uncontrollable wave of pacifism, and shortly afterwards the streets were resounding with the Russian equivalent of "Ave, Lenin!" . . .

In 1907, while the future autocrat was studying in Geneva, he used to attend the meetings of a society of Russian refugees. Although the subjects discussed by the members were chiefly political and economical, it was observed that Lenin, who always spoke well and knew his facts, invariably came to the meetings with a volume of Balzac, Hugo or De Maupassant under his arm. As newspapers and pamphlets were the stock reading of the other members, he was asked one evening how he got time to read what was vital when he always appeared to be indulging his literary whims. He replied:

"I study economics at night and history in the morning. The rest of my spare time is spent in observing human nature. De Maupassant and the rest of them tell me nearly everything that I have failed to find out for myself. The study of human nature, my friends, is more important for us than the study of political economy."

TWO DESPOTS

His own peculiar success vindicated the soundness of this judgment. . . .

A friend of mine was in prison at Astrakhan. He had been serving with Yudenitch and was captured during one of the latter's precipitate retreats. He could speak Russian fluently and had no difficulty in getting an interview with the local military governor, who eventually assented to the despatch of a letter to Lenin. This letter was to the effect that Captain —— (my friend) was an extremely important person and urgently requested a personal interview with the Dictator.

For several weeks he heard nothing, but at last a message came saying that he could proceed under a strong guard to headquarters. Within twenty-four hours of his arrival he was brought before Lenin, who received him genially and told the guard to retire. My friend was naturally amazed at such treatment and the conversation, which he reconstructed in English within an hour of its occurrence, was as follows :

CAPT : It's very kind of you to give me a private audience ; but how do you know I'm not going to assassinate you ?

LENIN : I don't know. Why do you want to see me ?

CAPT : I want a passport to England.

LENIN : In order to return and fight against us ?

CAPT : I shall have to obey my orders.

LENIN : Do you want to fight against us ?

CAPT : No.

LENIN : Then why return ?

CAPT : I am an Englishman.

LENIN : Would you like to go back to Yudenitch or to England ?

CAPT : You wouldn't let me go to Yudenitch.

LENIN : I might.

CAPT : Why ?

LENIN : Because you'd soon return to me. We've nearly finished with him.

CAPT : Then I'll go to England, please.

LENIN : You believe me, then ?

CAPT : Yes.

LENIN : I wish you could prevail upon your countrymen to do the same.

CAPT : They believe what they are told to believe.

LENIN : So do the Russians, but we tell them the truth.

CAPT : What is the truth ?

LENIN : Both sides of a question. . . . You will receive your passport shortly ; but I shan't send you home if you fight us again. Farewell.

A last story, more characteristic than any.

When the first serious counter-revolution was quelled by the Bolsheviks, its leader, a young man chiefly animated by hatred of Lenin, was tried and condemned to death. Lenin heard the result of the trial and sent an order to the court over-ruling it. At his suggestion the death-sentence on the young man was commuted to " twenty years faithfulness to his wife " (who was old enough to be his mother). That was Lenin to the life. . . .

§2

My second despot, Benito Mussolini, is (at any moment it may be " *was* ") a very different type. I have met him several times, and on each occasion I have found it difficult not to laugh outright. Everything he does is done for effect. He is one mass of poses, all of which have become so much a part of himself that a poseless Mussolini would now be almost an affectation ! In England he couldn't exist for ten minutes because his tricks, mannerisms and posturings would expose him to endless merriment.

But the Italians are a nation of actors. They love a good gesture, an imposing entrance, a dignified exit ; and the man who can bestride the boards like a Thespian is assured of their hysterical plaudits.

It is difficult for a phlegmatic Britisher like myself to overcome his natural aversion to histrionics, but I have seen enough of this kind of thing in my life to make me realize that it is not necessarily a sign of insincerity. Mussolini is far too great an egotist to be insincere, and his comicalities are so much a part of his temperament that if he suppressed them altogether he would probably go mad.

Besides, with it all there are many admirable traits in his character. Though he has exalted discipline into a sort of minor deity, he really is a freedom-lover at heart, believing that only in a perfectly-ordered State can true freedom exist. He has honestly tried to better the lot of the working-classes, and his ideal of a liberated and united Italy goes hand-in-hand with a passionate desire to make its people prosperous.

Primarily, however, he is a mummer like Napoleon —and could never be happy away from the limelight. In certain respects he plays his part more effectively than even Napoleon did. He knows the immense value of a silent salute. Above all he knows the value of silence, which Napoleon certainly didn't. A scene lingers in my memory and is noted fully in my diary.

There was a minor European crisis and half a dozen diplomatic representatives of the greater States had to meet him in council. I had met him before ; but this was the first time I had seen him away from the glare of the footlights, so to speak ; so now, if ever, I thought, the real man would show himself.

We were all chatting together on ordinary social matters when he made his entrance. I say " made his entrance " advisedly, because it was quite definitely a dramatic trick. Someone on the other side of the door by which we had entered opened it with a rattle and made a hissing sound, which seemed to suggest the advent of something exceptional. The door remained ajar and we all looked at it open-mouthed. There was a deathly silence, during which one could have heard that proverbial pin drop on to a piece of velvet.

" Good-morning, gentlemen."

We shot round. Mussolini was standing behind us, motionless. There was no sign of a door on that side of the room—and someone suggested, after we had left him, that he had come up through a trap-door, but I cannot verify this. Anyhow, there he was, smiling slightly, his eyes gleaming, his hand tucked into his breast-pocket, his pose sphinx-like, his face mask-like. As we looked at him he raised an arm, and the door by which he had not entered shut with such a sharp metallic snap that two of the most hardened diplomats present jumped from their seats.

Mussolini had addressed us in French and we returned his salutation in the same language. This done, there was a long silence while the Italian Prime Minister calmly scrutinized us, one by one. There was something extraordinarily rude about the way in which he conducted the business. Almost one heard him say to himself : " Now let me lay bare the souls of these ridiculous little people who imagine they are going to get the best of me."

Having inspected us thoroughly, he sat down with an alarming suddenness, which appeared all the more unusual because the expression on his face and the carriage of his body remained precisely the same as when he had been standing.

Another long silence was broken by someone

venturing the remark that we had better get to business. I can only describe what followed by saying that Mussolini *impaled* the speaker with a look that left him quivering, and, for the remainder of the session, practically speechless. The offender was of Latin stock and therefore susceptible to histrionic influences.

At last the Fascist leader, having duly impressed most of us, asked us to state the cases for our respective Governments. We did so with a brevity I have never known equalled and which I put down to the fact that our masterful host treated each of us, while we were speaking, to the most inquisitorial glare it had ever been my personal lot to withstand.

At the conclusion of our statements he said : " I thank you, gentlemen. You shall have my answer at ten minutes to four this afternoon."

I was about to ask him, with a triumphant touch of irony, whether twelve and a half minutes to four would be equally convenient, as I had an appointment at three and a quarter minutes past, when a more business-like colleague broke out with a " But——" He got no further. Mussolini rose from his seat with a terrifying celerity, barked a phrase in his native tongue that can only be translated colloquially as " ' But ' be damned ! " and gave two sharp taps on the table with his knuckles.

Instantly the door shot open ; two officers entered, saluted their chief, and stood aside for us to pass out. As we left his presence Mussolini was engaged in sniffing what might have been a bottle of smelling-salts—something at any rate that acted as an antidote to the atmosphere of six foreign diplomats, because we distinctly heard him say " That's better ! " as he held it to his nose.

Less than an hour later I received a message from him at my hotel begging me to visit him at once in the utmost secrecy. The diplomatic representative of France was with him when I arrived. At this interview he was quite a different man, affable, easy, natural and courteous. He explained that it was necessary to " impress " the majority of people, who loved being " fooled," but that with us he wished to deal quite frankly. Sometimes, he admitted with a smile, this duality of treatment caused a certain amount of inconvenience, but on the whole he thought it paid. He cited an instance when it had proved awkward.

During a slight misunderstanding with Turkey he had been forced in public to show the cold shoulder to a leading Turkish official—in order to keep up the appearance of strength. The Turk, in a huff, had promptly started home, and it was only by an accident that Mussolini heard of his departure in time to arrest his journey, bring him back to Rome, and apologize in private for the cavalier treatment he had received *coram populo*.

The Dictator then gave us the assurances we required for our two Governments, which were in every way satisfactory, and begged us to go through the formality of meeting him again with the others at ten minutes to four. We promised to do so. Then he gave us lunch and afterwards, in an elaborately roundabout manner, we returned to our hotels.

Three-fifty saw us back, with the other four, in the thaumaturgical apartment of the morning. Again the door was opened from without, and again a hissing sound proceeded from the corridor beyond ; but this time we were not to be taken in so easily and everyone of us turned from the door and looked in the other direction.

" Good-afternoon, gentlemen."

We spun round. Mussolini was smiling at us from the door. He pretended not to notice our annoyance, though the pleasure he felt at the success of his little trick was evident from the intensely provocative smirk of satisfaction that passed over his face.

Standing at the end of the table he then delivered a short and somewhat rhetorical address, which, while enabling all of us to comfort our Governments with the assurance that he would consult them in an emergency, nevertheless said fairly plainly that he must be given a perfectly free hand where Italian interests were concerned ; and since these interests were paramount in the present dispute, he did not anticipate an *inter*national emergency that would necessitate a consultation with the powers.

Two of us smiled inwardly. All of us frowned outwardly. Each of the four who had not seen him privately was mentally disentangling the flower of fact from the bush of his eloquence, when with a regal gesture Mussolini said " Gentlemen, you may deliberate "—and marched out of the room.

The gentlemen did not trouble to deliberate, because they knew it would be waste of time. So they went their several ways.

But since, in the long run, the assurances he gave to two of us in private were of no greater value than the discourse he gave to six of us in public, I am still deliberating as to whether the trap-door Mussolini or the tête-à-tête Mussolini is the better actor.

CHAPTER VII

CROWNS AND CORONETS

King George V, King Alfonso XIII, Queen Alexandra, Queen Mary, The Prince of Wales, The Duke of York, the ex-Crown Prince of Germany.

§1

A MATTER to which very few people give a second's consideration is the terrible and endless boredom of majesty. Unless a man is a born actor or has a colossal opinion of himself —much the same thing, by the way—he cannot possibly like being a king. The only monarch I have ever met who positively enjoyed his job was Kaiser Wilhelm ; but he, like all born actors, was eaten up with conceit.

As my readers are aware, King George V was not heir to the throne until he had attained manhood, and (of this my readers are *not* aware) the heirdom was a very bitter pill for him to swallow. Few men could ever have been so appalled at the prospect of kingship as George V. For years it lay like an ever-darkening shadow across the path of his daily life. He fought against this blighting menace with all his strength. Hardly a soul outside his immediate circle knew anything about the bitterness and intensity of that struggle.

He was not by nature a social man and he hadn't an atom of ambition. He pined for a peaceful life. The death of his elder brother, the Duke of Clarence, meant a great deal more to him than the death of a brother. It meant the death of his hopes. His wants were few. A trout stream, a moor, a wood or two, a select library, a few friends with whom he could discuss philosophy, science, the arts—that was all. Except for occasional bouts of indigestion, life seemed very pleasant to him in the year 1891.

Then came the crash, the shattering of all these pleasant dreams and domestic desires, and the long, long fight against an inherited yearning for privacy. His would be a strange story if it could be told. Of course it never can be; though I am able here to lift the veil for a moment, only to drop it again almost as soon as lifted. Hardly a hint of that uphill struggle escaped him. In a private letter of that period, which I have seen, a sigh is apparent here and there, but it is immediately suppressed and only a close personal friend could guess its true depth.

In the end duty conquered; and though the demon of an unutterable boredom is never far away, he has learnt to keep the horror at arm's length by a giant effort of the will.

I have seen him flinch before receiving an address.

I have seen him sink into an armchair after a civic function with an almost inaudible " Thank God that's over ! " I have noted the monotony creeping into his voice as he was losing interest in certain official proceedings and the sudden forced alteration of tone as he pulled himself together for a final spurt. And I have heard him speak, almost in tears of gratitude, of a certain minister of the Crown with whom he was in complete harmony.

To a colleague of mine he once unbosomed himself thus : " I could never be popular as my father was ; I haven't the right temperament." He spoke the words wistfully, and it was easy to see that he was not sorry on his own account but solely on account of the Crown. " However," he added thankfully, " my son more than makes up for my deficiencies."

He is interested in persons, not in politics ; and when the Labour Party came into power he was delighted—not because he agreed with their programme but because he was anxious to meet and know an entirely new set of people.

He would give anything to converse freely and equally with the leading writers of the time—Wells, Shaw, Galsworthy, Chesterton—but his necessary duties prevent it. " Those are the men," he once said to me, " who give the age its individuality ; they do not need any titles I could give them."

He rather dreads the flood of biographical and autobiographical work which is perhaps the most significant literary feature of his reign. "Where is it all going to stop?" he asked me. "Death is beginning to take on a new and far more terrifying aspect. It used to be feared," he continued with a smile; "now it should at all costs be avoided!" I don't think he much relished the introduction of the "John Brown" episode into Strachey's "Queen Victoria." And the story of King Edward arriving late for dinner, in the same book, was, he felt, somewhat "unnecessary."

He really dislikes horse-racing and would sacrifice a good deal in order to give free play to his disinclination in this respect. But as his chief distaste happens to be his chief social duty, he sets his teeth and does his job.

That, in brief, is both the triumph and the tragedy of King George V. By sheer force of will he has managed to lose the personality of the man in the performance of the marionette—but the plaudits gained by the latter bring him neither solace nor joy. . . .

§2

Another King who has come within my ken is Alfonso of Spain. I can best reveal his character by anecdote.

Several years ago it began to get about that Alfonso was in the habit of receiving certain of his ministers in private and "sounding" them on questions of policy. As a matter of fact, it was perfectly true, because Alfonso cannot rest unless he has a finger in every pie. But things came to a crisis when the rumour reached him that his conversations with one particular minister were being published broadcast. The point was : Who could be giving the show away ? The only person aware of these closely-closeted meetings was the King's own private secretary, and his discretion and loyalty were beyond all suspicion. So His Majesty made certain inquiries, and at his next informal talk with the minister in question he went straight to the point :

ALF : Of course you never breathe a word of our conversations to a soul.

MIN : Not a word.

ALF : It is absolutely between you and me.

MIN : Absolutely.

ALF : Not even your wife——

MIN : She is completely in ignorance of what passes between us.

ALF : Good. But in that case you must be more careful in your choice of a mistress.

The minister was dumbfounded and began to stammer. Alfonso realized that his shot had gone home—and from that moment the leakage ceased !

Alfonso's knowledge of his countrymen, and especially his countrywomen, is profound. In the same category as the last story is the following :

When the *coup d'état* which established the recent dictatorship was being planned, it was absolutely necessary that the King should be in constant communication with his co-plotters. Yet the reception of letters was dangerous, since his personal entourage could not always be trusted and information conveyed through the usual official channels was liable to go astray. He therefore arranged with Primo de Rivera and his lieutenants that all their confidential correspondence should be addressed personally to His Majesty's barber, who, when he arrived every morning to shave his royal master, delivered it into the King's hands. Alfonso was cute enough to perceive that a menial whose fortune has yet to be made is a safer recipient of secrets than a marquis whose fortune is in the balance!

Twenty-four hours before the stroke that was to decide the future of Spain, the King received, via his barber, a message from de Rivera begging him to have the movements of certain politicians then in power carefully watched, and urging him to take immediate action if any of them got wind of what was on foot. This was the King's laconic reply: "Have no fear. The mistresses of all the ministers you name are still in residence. We needn't watch the men till the women begin to pack-up."

That is one side of the man. There is another—and another. Let me illustrate them as concisely as I can.

Barcelona, as you may know, is the hotbed of the anarchist movement in Spain. Dozens of revolutionary clubs flourish there and very little is done to suppress them unless one or two begin to show symptoms of unpleasant activity.

Sometime in 1919 one of them manifested signs of eruption and the King was the chief object of its smouldering wrath. An attempt was made on his life, but it was frustrated in the nick of time, and the authorities decided to act. But the King at that moment was most anxious to preserve civil peace, and he sent for the officers in charge of the affair. To their astonishment he intimated his decision to attend in person a meeting of the club and to go unguarded. They expostulated, but nothing would turn him from his purpose. It was arranged, however, that a good force of armed police should be within call in case of need.

Two members of the club were already under arrest, and they had not only informed the police of the date and whereabouts of the next meeting, but had kindly (no doubt under slight suasion) given the necessary " Open Sesame " signal. Armed with the latter, the King arrived one evening outside a house in the suburbs of Barcelona, dressed in mufti.

He gave the correct knock, delivered the secret sign, and in a few minutes was standing among the malcontents. Their surprise deprived them of speech, because of course they recognized him at once. But he instantly put them as much at their ease as it is possible for revolutionaries to be by sitting down and asking if he might join in their deliberations that evening.

After their first gasp of amazement they settled down, as only Spaniards can, to an exhaustive debate on the political situation, the King getting just as heated in support of his government as they were in opposition to it. At length His Majesty wearied of the aimless argument and said :

" What you really want to do, then, is to end the present social system, and me with it, by force."

" Yes," cried a dozen voices.

" Then why not end me now ? " asked the King. " I've got to die sooner or later, and if you honestly think my death will benefit Spain, why not make it sooner ? " There was no reply. " But you do sincerely believe in force ? " pursued H.M. after a pause.

" Yes," again came in chorus.

" And so do I," chimed in Alfonso ; " so firmly indeed that I have arranged for this house to be surrounded by a force of police. Gentlemen, you will be my guests for a little while. When you have ceased to believe in force, I shall cease to employ it. Good-evening."

And the plucky young monarch walked out of the house, no one raising a finger to stop him. He kept his word. Every member of that club spent a period in gaol, long or short according to individual temperament. A written statement to the effect that he no longer believed in force was sufficient to gain the release of any one of them. I am told that the stoutest diehard stuck to his guns for two months.

Some of the facts I have recorded naturally got about and caused much merriment. It was a case of ridicule killing a revolution. . . .

One other aspect of Alfonso's character, not quite so attractive as those I have just sketched.

He was discussing the Riff campaign with a general who was on temporary leave from the war zone. The King couldn't understand why certain movements of troops which he himself had ordered should have failed to secure their objective. The general temporized, feeling himself on delicate ground, since a criticism might have reflected on the wisdom of the order.

Alfonso, who is nothing if not direct, rapped out a whole series of questions—" Why this ? " " Why that ? " " Why the other thing ? " The general was flustered and began once more to hedge ; but the King in a rage hit the table at his side and shouted : " Why ? Why ? *Why?* I command you to tell me."

Thereupon the general flung discretion to the winds and blurted out : " It was impossible to carry out your instructions in full. The value of the strategical gain would not have compensated for the loss of life."

Alfonso went livid. There was an appalling silence. Then he hissed out the words :

" My orders must be obeyed to the letter, *whatever the consequences.*"

The general bowed low and retired. Shortly after

he was dismissed from the service under circumstances of peculiar ignominy which I am afraid were manufactured for the purpose. No wonder he prays in exile for " a day of retribution," that will include in its programme certain bloody actions of a retaliatory nature !

§3

It is difficult to account for the strange halo of sanctity that the general public bestow upon people around whose personalities some sort of tradition has sprung up. It would almost seem as if the mere fact of growing old entitled them to a place among the saints. In my own time I have seen the halo growing in size year by year upon such a strange assortment of heads as those of Florence Nightingale, Thomas Hardy, Lord Roberts and Ellen Terry. As a consequence the popular idea of all such folk becomes hopelessly distorted ; indeed, the biographies that are written about them are so far away from the truth that their closest friends wouldn't recognize the enhaloed subjects unless their names appeared on the title-pages !

Lytton Strachey has corrected the current conception of Florence Nightingale. And possibly some future Strachey will give a truthful portrait of Queen Alexandra. My few notes will, I hope, help him to that end.

In her case nothing could be further from the truth than the popular picture of a gentle, patient, uncomplaining lady who wouldn't have dreamt of saying " Bo " to a goose. Yet that is the accepted belief—which I must now proceed to shatter.

One day in the year 1904 she was glancing down the list of people who were to be presented at the next " Court." Her eye caught the name of a lady then famous in social circles of whom she did not approve. She promptly erased the name, and began to give the list her closest attention. The result of her scrutiny was the erasure of six more names. She then returned the list to the proper quarter, with a written order that no invitations should be sent to the names she had crossed out.

A nervous official waited upon her next morning and begged her to reconsider the inclusion of the seven names, since they had been added at the express desire of King Edward.

" Under no circumstances whatever will I consent to receive them," said the Queen; " and if His Majesty has anything further to say, he can say it to me."

Trembling visibly the official withdrew and informed Lord Knollys of the occurrence. The latter reported the incident to the King. And His Majesty had nothing further to say !

On another occasion, when she was Princess of Wales, a statement appeared in a London daily paper which she could only regard as a personal affront. Sir Dighton Probyn was detailed to handle this delicate matter, and went down to see the editor.

The latter "could not see his way" to issue a démenti of the statement. After trying every possible line of argument, Sir Dighton begged the editor to visit Her Royal Highness. The editor refused point-blank, and Sir Dighton was forced to end the discussion.

Within an hour a private carriage drew up at the office of the offending periodical, a thickly-veiled lady got out and demanded to see the editor on urgent private business, giving her name as the Baroness of R——. She did not leave the office until she had "passed for press" a certain paragraph —for the insertion of which the type had to be reset —that rendered innocuous another paragraph that had appeared in a previous issue. When she had satisfied herself that the business was settled and had received the profuse apologies of the editor, the Princess of Wales drove back to Marlborough House. . . .

Shortly after one of my official visits to Germany I had the honour of an interview with Queen Alexandra. Almost before a word of formality had passed between us, she broke out with:

"Now tell me what you really think of them."

"Them?" I questioned.

"Yes, the Germans."

"I liked them," I said.

"Seriously?"

"Seriously, your Majesty."

"What a disappointment!"

"Disappointment?"

" Yes, I detest them ! "

This rather took me aback. Then I remembered the Schleswig-Holstein affair, and said : "Naturally."

" Oh, I'm not only thinking of '66 ! " she exclaimed—" it's their self-love I can't bear. Sometimes when Wilhelm is talking I could almost scream. They're all like that—the Prussians, I mean—and nearly all our relations are thoroughly Prussianized now. You can have no idea how difficult I find it to be polite to them. D'you think they'd beat us in a war ? "

" It will never come to that," said I. " They wouldn't dare attack England and France together."

" Don't be so sure," said the Queen, shaking a finger at me ; " in their own opinion they're unbeatable, so why should they fear the Entente Cordiale ? "

" They have a lot of commonsense," was all I could find to say.

" Commonsense indeed ! " flared up Her Majesty ; " I never knew a nation with less of it." Then, suddenly breaking off, she cried : " Oh, wouldn't it be glorious if our dear little England could beat that nation of swaggerers ! "

Her eyes shone as she spoke the words. And Germany was not the only goose to which Queen Alexandra said " Bo " during that half-hour's conversation !

§4

There is not much of her mother-in-law about Queen Mary, though curiously enough the average view of her is that she is more than a little autocratic. I have only met her twice and on both occasions she gave me the impression of being supremely happy, as of one who was wholly at peace with herself and in complete harmony with her surroundings.

The present Prince of Wales once told me that his mother had the knack of compelling obedience without effort—as if she herself were so sure of what was right that no one ever for a moment questioned her commands. And he also told me that when he or his sister or any of his brothers were in need of advice, they never dreamt of going to anyone for it but their mother. Even the King would rather depend upon her instinctive wisdom than upon that of his personal advisers. Scores of times she has helped him out of momentary difficulties by prompting him with a right word or suggesting a tactful action on the spur of the moment. She is never at a loss for a new idea when a previously-rehearsed incident or speech has had to be omitted in favour of something else or adapted to the exigencies of the moment.

Withal she is a great stickler for etiquette. There is a proper way to do everything, in her opinion, and she is an adept at the art of signifying displeasure whenever anything is done amiss. The best instance

I can give of this took place at Windsor during a dinner to which I and several colleagues of the Diplomatic Corps had been invited.

A well-known Ambassador, since dead, was airing his views on the population question. Among other things he remarked that the poor of every nation should be prevented from adding to the load of misery in the world by producing larger families than they could support.

" As the poor are not here to defend themselves," said Queen Mary with a smile, " I think we had better leave them out of the discussion "—which was a very polite way of telling the Malthusian to change this debatable subject, and had its effect.

But she is quite capable of giving a much sharper rap over the knuckles than that. For once, when a certain lady had importuned her to use her influence for the advancement of a favourite son, Her Majesty answered :

" When he has done anything to deserve it, he will not need my influence."

Lord Milner was very fond of describing a passage of arms between King George and Queen Mary at which he had been present. The dispute was over a certain novel. After several thrusts from the King, who didn't like the book, and parries from the Queen, who did, His Majesty summed up: " Well, I can't think what you find in it to admire." To which Her Majesty laconically replied: " Nor can I, but I do."

This very accurately paints Her Majesty's leading characteristic. She can seldom find reasons for her beliefs. She simply *feels* a thing is so or is not so. She implicitly trusts her instincts, and no amount of argument will persuade her to think them wrong.

§5

Brothers are notoriously unlike one another, but I doubt if any two brothers were ever less alike than the Prince of Wales and the Duke of York.

The Prince is an extraordinarily interesting human study. I can do no more than glance at a few traits here, feeling fairly confident that he will one day be the subject of an absorbing biography. I don't mean the usual and apparently inevitable two volumes of official praise, which will do its best to bury his personality, but a rattling good book after the Strachey pattern.

His curious temperament expresses itself in all sorts of directions, but in none more persistently than in an unquenchable eagerness to talk to everybody he meets. It is this incessant talkativeness that has made him so popular wherever he goes; because he chats to a dustman with every bit as much relish and abandon as to a duke—in fact, if anything, he prefers conversation with the dustman. His democratic amiability has resulted in some queer misunderstandings, many of which have already found their way into print.

He, I may say, is very downright in his opinions of others and would be the last person in the world to object to a frank portrait of himself.

Another aspect of his character that makes him strangely unlike his ancestors is his utter disregard of etiquette. His friends address him very much as they like, and such expressions as " old bean " and " old sport " are common in his circle. Also he doesn't seem to mind what he wears, though he is always admirably " groomed."

At a big meeting of hospital directors he turned up to take the chair in a morning suit, blue shirt, blue collar, and several other unbusiness-like colours. One of the directors whispered to another : " He'll be coming in his ' shaver ' next." The Prince overheard it and, to the unutterable consternation of his critic, whispered back : " I shall."

All of which proves that for a democratic age like ours he is the right man in the right place. And in England especially he would make a thoroughly representative monarch; because on every State occasion he would give anything to take off his crown and play football with it !

§6

The Duke of York has never flung himself headlong into the stream of life. He prefers to remain on the bank and peer critically into the depths beyond. Everything about him is ordered and careful—from his guarded conversation to his sober demeanour. No one would dream of clapping him on the back ; nor would he dream of taking that liberty with anyone else.

I have heard him talk to a minister of the Crown for something like an hour, and not once did he advance a personal opinion definite enough for the other to say " The Duke of York thinks so-and-so." He is the essence of discretion and nothing could induce him to " give himself away." His policy throughout life is to have no policy—or at least, if he has one, to keep it to himself. " Take each man's censure but reserve thy judgment " is the keynote of his character.

He is strangely unreceptive to outside influences, dead to a sense of popular feeling. In the war he would have made a good staff-officer but a bad mess-mate—again the reverse of his brother, who was a poor staff-officer and a perfect mess-mate. On one occasion the Duke was advised to act in a particular manner.

" Why ? " he asked.

" It would be a gracious thing to do."

" Gracious ? " he said.

" Yes—popular."

" Oh ! " he exclaimed somewhat ruefully; " I thought there was a reason for it."

Another time a large number of seats had been reserved for him and his friends at a football match. When he turned up it was noticed that only half

the seats reserved for his party were occupied; and
as thousands of people couldn't gain admission for
lack of accommodation, it was hinted that the empty
seats in his neighbourhood should be filled by the
general public. But the hint was lost upon him—
not because he was too selfish to take it, but because
he was too "distant" to notice it.

A good deal of this aloofness and unresponsiveness
to atmosphere is due to a natural timidity which
literally amounts to torture. Public speaking is
an agony to him, and it led him on a certain
occasion to make one of those rare outbursts,
a veritable *cri de cœur*, to which in the ordinary way
he is an absolute stranger : "I wish the earth would
open and swallow me up."

Though utterly dissimilar in temperament, as I
have said, the Duke is devoted to his elder brother.
It is a case of extremes meeting and unlikes liking
one another. But if you were to ask him why the
Prince is so popular he would reply : "Because he's
such a cheery fellow." Thereby again proving his
insensitiveness to such matters as personality, adapta-
bility to surroundings, and the value of effective
gestures.

Conscientious, painstaking, upright, idealistic, with
a high conception of public duty, a keen sense of
personal honour, and a desperate desire to do the
right thing in the right way, he is more like that
other Duke of York, who afterwards became
James II, than any other of our royal princes. And,

I may add, the last of the Stuart kings has never
yet had justice done him. . . .

§7

In startling contrast with King George's elder
children is (or perhaps I should say *was*, as I haven't
seen him since 1914) the ex-Crown Prince of Germany.
He may have altered since the war. He probably
has—for he is nothing if not changeable. One could
never be sure of his mood for ten minutes together.
Quite the funniest *volte-face* I ever witnessed in my
life was exhibited by him during a hunt in the Black
Forest.

Someone had brought him a long envelope, the
contents of which put him in a towering temper.
He turned on one of his secretaries and literally
petrified the poor fellow with curses. He stormed
and stamped and went crimson with rage, treating
his victim to a whirlpool of verbal frenzy and a
shower-bath of foam. Meanwhile the lady with
whom he had previously been speaking stood close
at hand waiting for the storm to blow over. With
a final spit and a vigorous kick he turned from his
wretched subordinate. At the same second his eyes
lit upon the lady, and as they did so the expression
on his face instantly turned from one of livid fury
to one of smiling delight. His voice changed its
tone of guttural brutality and became suave and almost
musical. As they passed me he was chatting away

with a charming insouciance that made me rub my eyes and wonder whether he was the same man who a moment ago had behaved like an angry bear or a raving lunatic.

His variableness of mood sometimes took the quaintest forms. During his visit to India the people who had to entertain him were frequently quite nonplussed by his behaviour and eventually it became necessary to appoint certain army officers to attend him wherever he went; not merely as a matter of courtesy, for he was invariably trying to evade them, but chiefly to keep an eye on him, set a limit to his actions, and curb his reckless desire for adventure.

He loved going down into the native quarter of a town—for reasons, I must add, not wholly ethnological—and as his disappearances sometimes coincided with official functions that were held in his honour, the authorities were driven to distraction. Once, after he had been missing for several hours and the native quarter had been thoroughly " dragged," he was found gravely consulting some learned Mussulman in a mosque. Official India gasped and he was begged not to do it again.

The Kaiser, of course, never knew what he would be up to next, and was several times forced to put him under lock and key—by which I mean that he was confined to the house and grounds of some castle or other. His periods of contrite penitence alternated so swiftly with those other periods of utter indulgence that at length his father gave it up as a hopeless job and let him have a free rein.

An amusing instance of the Crown Prince's weathercock temperament occurred while I was staying in Berlin. He had been summoned to the Kaiser's presence to answer for a misdemeanour that threatened to burst into a public scandal. The possibility of such an event had so cowed the Crown Prince that his expressions of sorrow were sincere and heartfelt, and when Wilhelm read him a long lecture on his conduct he burst into tears and implored his father's forgiveness.

The latter was delighted to behold this most becoming and unlooked-for state of resipiscence in his heir and instantly extended his parental absolution. (This, by the way, took place before the offender had allowed punctual penitence to develop into a habit.) Piously murmuring his humble gratitude, the Crown Prince took his leave. It now only remained for him to make his profound apologies to a certain gentleman who was even then quivering with rage and indignation in his Berlin residence. The Prince drove down to the gentleman's house and was ushered into his presence. But he had already had time to forget his tears, and instead of apologizing he loaded the other with reproaches for daring to take his troubles to the Kaiser. He then turned on his heel and walked out.

The Kaiser was furious when he heard what had happened, and again summoned the Crown Prince to his presence. But the latter refused to obey and trotted off to the Riviera, after despatching a letter to his imperial father in which he exhorted him to thank God for a son who upheld the honour of the Hohenzollerns at the cost of a personal exposure ! . . .

The Prince's idea of honour was, you will note, a stubborn refusal to apologize to a man he had insulted, because that man was inferior in class and prestige to himself. It is an idea common to the snobs of all races and all ages. What made it quaintly characteristic in his case was that a month later, when he had a boon to beg of his father, he forgot all about the honour of the Hohenzollerns and apologized to the gentleman he had wronged with tears in his eyes.

CHAPTER VIII

SCRIBBLERS

*H. G. Wells, Bernard Shaw, Thomas Hardy, Henry
James, Rudyard Kipling, Mark Twain.*

§1

MY life has been almost wholly passed in
the midst of big events and amongst the
leading actors, the controlling agents, of
those events. I have had little time to spare for
fireside critics or fireside caterers. By the former
I mean the sociologists, by the latter the novelists.

Sometimes, though, I have come into personal
contact with these zealots for reform, these contrivers
of situations, these pseudo-psychologists, these word
spinners, these jabberers on a mimic stage. Nearly
all of them suffer from the curious delusion that they
could run the universe better than those who do
run it. Most of them are charming fellows who
wouldn't harm a fly, though some of their writings
seem to suggest that they would like to impale
humanity.

Affecting, for the most part, to despise society,
they find it difficult to refuse an invitation from a

duchess—and in that way we whom they criticize or pretend to scorn are brought into touch with them.

On arrival at one of these affairs my hostess bustled up to me and said : " Oh, you must know H. G. Wells ! He's coming to-night. Do tell me what you think of him. He's not ' quite quite,' you know, but he's so clever." And in this manner I met the prophet of the cosmos.

I thought his manner remarkably taking. He has a distinct flair for making conversation sound important. And he keeps the ball of genial generalities rolling with masterly adroitness. But he undoubtedly suffers from a sense of thwarted ambition. He would give his head to be a commanding influence in the world of action, and he writhes inwardly at the destiny that condemns him to the impotence of the ink-pot. This accounts for his childish attacks on such big historical figures as Napoleon, Cæsar, etc. He envies their halo of heroism ; and, in the one good phrase that psycho-analysis has given us, he is the victim of an " inferiority complex."

Not unnaturally he is somewhat embittered and when his conversation descends from the general to the particular he is liable to become almost as " catty " as a spinster of advancing years who has been jilted by the curate.

But somehow even his acidity does not detract from his personal charm, and I can quite understand why he is so popular with the other sex. His neat hands and small feet, his frankness of address, flow of ideas and freedom from pose, above all his immediate responsiveness and intuitive sympathy ; here are sufficient causes for feminine adoration without that final cause of causes—the glamour of success.

In this connection I was amused to note that while we talked together his eye went roaming about the room, now and then alighting upon some female beauty with the appreciative pause of a connoisseur. He was quite able to indulge his search for pretty faces without for a moment losing his mental grip on the subject we were discussing, therein proving more than a match for me, for I find that my mind usually takes flight with my conscious eye.

His voice is by no means pleasant—certain notes grate upon one's ear—and it is without volume. Also he does not know how to use it. Which alone proves the exceptional attractiveness of his other qualities, since nothing can be so alluring or so offensive as a voice.

This brief summary of the man found its way into my diary within a few hours of our meeting, together with the following anecdote.

In the course of our talk an acquaintance of his joined us with the words :

" I say, Wells, when are you going to give us another ' Kipps ' ? "

I could see from the expression on his face that Wells had been subjected to this sort of thing before.

" Isn't one enough ? " he countered.

" You can't beat it," pursued the other ; " that's your style right enough—the shabby genteel."

Though the fellow meant no harm and was only trying to be chattily jocular, this last thrust went home and made Wells wince.

" Glad you recognize it," was all he said, and went on conversing with me. But the other chap was not to be shaken off so easily.

" Can't you give all this propaganda stuff a rest for a bit," he persisted, " and give us another good laugh ? "

" So long as the majority of people prefer laughing to thinking," came Wells's retort, " they'll get nothing but propaganda from me. Besides," he added quickly, as he observed the other was about to continue the topic, " I don't know that I was sent into the world to make people laugh, when not a few of them make me want to cry."

This effectually silenced the laughter lover ; but, not to take any risks, Wells turned rapidly to me and continued our conversation with a very pointed " As I was saying. . . ."

§2

I met Bernard Shaw at a big " crush " at Sir Philip Sassoon's place in Park Lane about two years before the war. Seldom have I seen a man so utterly lost in his surroundings. When I first caught sight of him he was standing in the middle of one of the reception rooms glancing from right to left in a most agitated manner, as though trying to find a way of escape. He was in full rig, which struck me as curious, because I had always heard he refused to wear orthodox evening apparel.

I observed that whenever he spotted anyone bearing down upon him he fled in an opposite direction. Once he was forced to quit the room altogether and nearly fell into the arms of a lady who was waiting for him in the hall outside. Pretending not to see her, he retrieved the position by retiring hurriedly to the room he had just left through another door. But here his good angel deserted him utterly, for the person he had previously tried to dodge had been observing his tactics in the hall beyond and was ready for him. Hopelessly cornered, Shaw took out his watch, said "How are you? I'm looking for Granville Barker. Have you seen him?" all in one breath, and without waiting for an answer, did a sprint across the room and out through the opposite door.

I was so intrigued by his antics that I followed him and watched him threading his way through a crowd of people who were tackling refreshments at odd tables about the floor. Suddenly he caught sight of Barker in a corner and made a bee-line for him. But it was a dangerous thing to do, as he found to his cost. His retreat to both doors was now completely cut off, a fact that was not lost on a stoutish lady wearing a diamond tiara and bedecked with jewels of many colours.

She promptly closed in upon him, and he had only just managed to utter the words " Barker, I can't stand any more of this, I'm off," when her fan commenced a tattoo on his back.

It would be difficult to describe the expression on his face when he realized that all was lost. A baffled look, a bewildered look, a beseeching look : these and something more ; something that suggested a keen appreciation of the absurdity and futility of the lady in the tiara, of himself—and pretty well everything else. But all would be lost indeed if Shaw were lost for a longer time than it takes to say " Oh ! " Following the expressions I have tried to describe, following them so quickly that Barker had only just replied " I shall be leaving shortly, too," came another expression which I can only characterize as one of seraphic benignity.

Patting her hand with a warmth of welcome that it would seem impossible to simulate, Shaw graciously introduced her to Barker, adding the words, " He is dying to make your acquaintance "—and only just restrained himself from executing a *pas seul* out of sheer delight as he vanished from their view.

That, I thought, was the last I would see of Mr. Shaw. But I was mistaken. Upon returning to the room where I had first seen him, to my intense surprise I beheld him in close colloquy with a man who might have been one of the servants but for

the fact that his dress-clothes were nothing like as
smart as theirs. He had a weary-looking countenance
and a drooping demeanour. I noticed, too, that he
had a fixed and tired smile on his face, probably in
order to save himself the trouble of relaxing his
features whenever Shaw made a joke. (It is a
curious thing, by the way, that when a man gets a
reputation for being funny, people who meet him
usually start smiling before he starts speaking.)

Shaw was certainly doing his best on this occasion
to deserve the smile, and was busy making up for
the other's languid humour by roaring with laughter
at his own remarks. As I passed them Shaw
happened to mention his companion by name. It
was John Masefield. I had read some of his work,
and I must say that his poems have nothing in
common with his profile. . . .

A few minutes later I was leaving the house when
who should I pass on the steps but G. B. S. It was
raining and he was in difficulties with his gamp.

" Can I give you a lift ? " said I.

" That's very nice of you," he returned, " but I
live right out of the way."

I told him I was in no hurry and that nothing
would give me greater pleasure than to drop him
at Charing Cross Station, near which, as he said, he
lived. He accepted my invitation, and we were soon
cutting along Piccadilly.

" I'm afraid," I said, " that I have the advantage
of you. Sir Philip pointed you out to me, and——"

" Wrong," he interrupted ; " I know you better than you know me. I've read at least three of your despatches right through, which is more than you've ever done to one of my Prefaces ! "

" *You*'re wrong this time," I cried ; " I've read four of your books from cover to cover and seen several of your plays into the bargain."

" Then that absolves me from treating you with respect," he replied with a laugh.

" I don't mind your not treating me with respect in the least," I said, " but I hardly see——"

" Let me explain," he broke in ; " I am nothing if not explanatory."

So I shut my mouth while he discoursed :

" People who read my Prefaces are repelled by what they choose to term my arrogance—their word for my habit of telling the painful truth. And people who read what other folk say about me are revolted by my callousness—the average journalist's word for the irritating way in which I keep my head while the rest of mankind are losing theirs. Thus everyone who doesn't know me firmly believes me to be quite the most unpleasant person alive ; and as a consequence all I have to do with people who meet me for the first time is to be just reasonably polite, in order to convey an impression of superhuman charm."

" I don't quite see what that has to do with your not treating me with respect," I argued.

" Oh, that's quite another matter ! " exclaimed

Shaw, who had obviously clean forgotten what he intended to speak about the moment he opened his mouth. " If you have read my books you won't expect me to behave like an ordinary human being. Lots of people who know me only as a private individual, without any suspicion of that newspaper bogey ' G. B. S.', are amazed when they discover in some accidental manner that I am a red-hot socialist —which to them is something far less explicable than a murderer ! They can't understand how a revolutionist can be a respectable—indeed, a highly respectable—member of society. And, as a matter of fact, they flatly decline to believe I am one—even after they have forced me to acknowledge my creed. But you, having read my works, know me for what I truly am, and you are doubtless wondering why I don't seize you by the throat or jump out of the car or do some equally senseless thing that would, in your opinion, brand me as the villain I profess to be."

I thanked him for his good opinion of my intelligence ; whereat he laughed and said that after a " social evening " a man should be forgiven anything.

" I am not in the least surprised," he added, " that people drink too much at these appalling functions. If I went in for them regularly I would quickly become an incurable dipsomaniac. Perhaps the sort of people who go to them can only endure one another drunk. Certainly most of them would be much more interesting in a condition of delirium tremens."

With which kindly reflection on the possibility of

improvement in the human species, he stepped lightly from the car, waved his hand, and disappeared beneath his umbrella. . . .

§3

Thomas Hardy is the highbrow's hero. Yet he has managed to survive it. Which may be due to the fact that he has never encouraged highbrows. If anything, indeed, he has repelled their advances. At carefully-timed intervals they find their way to Dorchester, only to be told that the G.O.M. is not well enough to see them. Actually he is sunning himself among the rose-trees in the back-garden and simply does not want to be pestered by them. Come one, come all! He daren't risk it. Besides, he never is well enough to see *them*. Half an hour of their society would go far to kill his still-flowering muse. It would be as much as his work was worth.

So the remarkable old gentleman remains hidden among his rose-trees. This necessary seclusion makes the hearts of his disciples beat all the faster. They look up at the house and marvel at its strangely suburban architecture. They rhapsodize on the contrast between the prim retreat and its primitive occupant. And when they return home they reverently insert a flower, plucked surreptitiously from a garden-border watered (they hope) by the master's own hand, between the pages of " Jude the Obscure."

Had they been fortunate enough to catch him

unawares, before he had received warning of their approach and beaten a hasty retreat, they would have marvelled still more at the contrast between the hero of their imaginations and the quaint individual who welcomes them in a businesslike manner, refuses to talk about literature, and insists upon discussing the price of ducks or the present state of agriculture.

The great Wessex novelist is not in any sense a typical literary man. If he had been, I would not have enjoyed a certain week-end which I had the good fortune to spend in his house half as much as I did. In chatting to this amiable and matter-of-fact country-man, few would guess him to be a writer of inter-national renown. He is, most refreshingly, an ordinary mortal, keenly interested in the everyday matters that absorb the attention of other ordinary mortals.

Even the Prince of Wales failed to " draw " him on the subject of his own works ; they discussed the war, the weather, the Empire, the harvest, the trade-depression, the scenery, local folk-lore—every-thing in fact except the Wessex novels. For the famous writer is big enough to forget Thomas Hardy.

All the same one can't escape from the fact that this man one is talking to is indeed the author of " Tess " and the rest of them. He sees life clearly, but he does not see it wholly. His outlook is dismal. He sees men and women as so many jokes of a jeering deity. One remark he made I shall never forget.

It sums him up and it sums his books up ; and the fact that I remember it so vividly—for I did not jot it down at the time—is proof that he is not a man of epigrams but rather a man of one enormous epigram, which can only be repeated in different forms. Speaking of mankind generally, this is how he delivered himself :

" Fate stalks us with depressing monotony from womb to tomb, and, when we are least expecting it, deals us a series of crushing blows from behind. Though the rays of intermittent happiness are permitted to play upon us for our greater undoing, we are marked down for miserable ends."

That phrase " *from womb to tomb* " gave me the whole of Thomas Hardy. There was something so fatally ineluctable about it. Coming from the mouth of that pleasant old gentleman, it seemed strangely incongruous and yet the absolute epitome of life. It included the writer and all his works, the doer and all his deeds. . . .

§4

Some artists use words to express thoughts. Others use words to express—words ! Henry James was one of the others. He suffered from logomania. He was so obsessed with the choice and placing of words that his own conversation was affected. I sometimes used to wonder why he talked at all, because he could never rest content with the phrases that came to his tongue. He simply couldn't leave the English language alone. He would extract a word from his verbal storehouse, drop it, substitute another, than a third, and so on until he had constructed a veritable pyramid of synonyms. Hamlet's speech " To be or not to be " would in his hands have been expanded into an essay as long as " Hamlet." The essence of his form was formlessness. He spent his life in trying to disentangle himself from a maze of his own making.

This terrible word-malady used to break out in the most ludicrous fashion on all sorts of occasions. I was lunching with him once at Princes Restaurant, and this is how he asked the waiter to get him a chop :

" Bring me . . . . fetch me . . . . carry me . . . . supply me . . . . in other words (I hope you are following me) serve—when it is cooked . . . . scorched . . . . grilled, I should say—a large . . . . considerable . . . . meaty (as opposed to fatty) . . . . chop. . . ."

The waiter departed on his errand, though I observed that he consulted a friend on his way out—probably as to the wisdom of catering for eccentrics.

But the most remarkable instance of James's phrase-fad in my experience was reserved for another occasion. Before recording it I would like to mention that a young journalist of my acquaintance once asked me to give him an anecdote for publication. I gave him this, which he sent to the editors of three papers. Not one of them believed it, which only goes to show that truth is much stranger than the

fiction with which they entertain their readers. I
will now set forth the incident exactly as it occurred.
The morning papers were full of the death of
George Meredith, and I had been talking about it
to a friend at the Athenæum. Suddenly I remembered an important appointment, excused myself
hurriedly and walked out of the club. I had got
as far as Pall Mall when I recollected that I had left
my umbrella behind. I turned and ran back to the
club, dashed up the steps, and rammed a portly
gentleman who was standing just beyond the door
in the pit of the stomach. I was too flurried at the
moment to realise who it was, so I stammered out
my apologies and was just about to continue my
journey when my arm was gripped by the portly one.
"My dear fellow . . . . chap . . . . boy . . . ."
said he ; "where are you going ? Whither away so
fast ? Why this haste . . . . this indecorous speed ?
Is it an alarm or merely an excursion . . . . *in*cursion,
I should say . . . . forgive me . . . . Or has it . . . . .
is it . . . . anything to do with the lamentable . . . .
melancholy . . . . sorrowful . . . . doomful . . . . day-
eclipsing . . . . thought-paralyzing . . . . news . . . .
information . . . . bulletin . . . . in this morning's
journals . . . . papers . . . . sheets . . . . ? "
Long before this I had recovered my breath,
recognized the portly gentleman as Henry James, and
decided to cut short the interview at peril of his
displeasure.
"Yes, it's dreadful, isn't it ? " I said.

" The . . . . the . . . . the . . . ." he began.

" I'm awfully sorry, but I simply must go," I chipped in ; " I returned to fetch my umbrella. I've a most important appointment. Please forgive me for bumping into you "—and I made as if to leave him. But he held me fast and began again :

" The . . . . the death . . . . demise . . . . decease . . . . bodily-defection . . . . of George Meredith . . . . fills me with despair . . . . anguish . . . . distress . . . . unspeakable grief . . . . It would be impossible . . . . unthinkable . . . . inconceivable . . . . to dare to express my (shall I say it ?) my . . . ."

" No ! " I exclaimed, interrupting him quickly ; " no, I beg that you won't. I quite understand, I assure you. I quite——" but that was as far as I got.

" You quite understand ? How can you *quite* understand feelings . . . . sensations . . . . mute . . . . dumb . . . . which even I (is it not so ?) fail to comprehend . . . . which pass the bounds (am I wrong ?) of rigid expression ? "

Each dip into the dictionary had been punctuated by a hard intake of the breath ; but here he paused, searched me with his eyes, wrenched at my arm, and left me with the impression that he had expected me throughout to come along with the right word the moment he had exhausted all the wrong ones, and that I had failed miserably in my duty. Just as I was about to protest against my enforced and

rather painful captivity, he extinguished me with
another etymological effort :

" *Such* a thing as the passing . . . . the (shall we
call it ?) soul-delivery of our old friend can hardly
be . . . . can scarcely be . . . . can with difficulty be
thought upon in the (forgive me) rush . . . . tumble
. . . . and indeed scurry of everyday affairs, however
pressing, however unnecessarily and (perhaps) un-
premeditatedly crude . . . . possibly even (you must
overlook this) rude. . . ."

I was naturally fidgetting to get away from him
all the while, a fact that he was fully aware of but
rather appeared to resent. At the word " rude " I
opened my mouth and was on the point of asking
him politely to free my arm when, with a wide and
regal gesture, he cast me from him with the words :

" It will not rain, but you may fetch your umbrella
. . . your . . . . your *impedimenta* . . . ."

§5

In the whole course of my varied experience of
all sorts and conditions of men in all sorts and conditions of places, I have never met a person who is
the prey of so many contradictory moods as Rudyard
Kipling. I have sat next to him twice at dinner,
have smoked a pipe with him on a cross-channel
steamer, have compared Indian impressions with
him at Rottingdean, and have talked commonplaces
with him on at least six other chance occasions—but

it is safe to say that I have never known him twice alike.

Sometimes he is wholly delightful, giving himself up entirely to the social interchanges of the moment ; sometimes he is thoughtful and can only be induced to take part in a discussion with the greatest difficulty ; sometimes he is morose, and then he will snub anyone who breaks in upon his mood ; sometimes he is dreamy and will monologize by the hour on fairies and tales of long ago ; and sometimes he is in a martial vein, when he will argue about everything with a vehemence that leaves his opponents gasping.

Thus people who have met him once, twice, or even thrice, know less about him than those who have never clapped eyes on him ; and I have listened to a heated argument between a man and a woman in which the latter has insisted that he is the most perfect gentleman and the most ideal companion in the world, while the former has called him with equal conviction the very opposite. When I told them that, in my opinion, they were both right, they treated me for the remainder of the session with an indulgence usually bestowed upon a congenital idiot.

I will give you a few instances of Kipling's— what shall I call it ?—moodiness.

He was present at a big social gathering in Bombay, and was mildly peering about from under that beetling brow of his when an acquaintance came up behind him, slapped him heartily on the back, and seized his hand before he could say a word.

"I have been looking for you all over the place," cried the acquaintance.

"And I have been looking for you all over the place," muttered Kipling.

"Then we are both satisfied," said the other.

"Not at all," returned Kipling; "I was anxious to keep out of your way."

As the famous author is able to convey his meaning by his manner just as easily as by his matter, the acquaintance did not stop for further parley. . . .

I remember a dinner at which he was a guest, and the conversation happened to turn upon dogs. To the manifest delight of a certain lady sitting opposite him, Kipling began to hold forth on the glories of the canine nature. In fact he praised them so fulsomely that I wondered what humanity had done to be left out in the cold, for he couldn't have lauded his best friend in more glowing terms.

The lady opposite beamed upon him and gushed with platitudes of approbation. For a month afterwards she could speak of nothing but Mr. Kipling's brilliant discernment and beauty of character. Then suddenly his name disappeared totally from her meal-time conversation and everyone wondered what had happened. At last the truth leaked out. Kipling had passed her in Hyde Park. She had called after him and he had slowly retraced his steps. After shaking hands, she effusively, he glumly, there was a long pause. She couldn't understand his silence, for, standing so prettily at her feet in statuesque immobility, were her two pet Poms—ineffable representatives of that flawless tribe which he had praised so lyrically. At length she could remain in speechless anticipation no longer :

" What do you think of the little darlings ? " she asked with suppressed emotion and a loving glance at the two motionless creatures at her side.

" I think that you have an admirable taxidermist," answered Kipling, " though possibly his taste is a trifle effeminate."

Which may also have had something to do with the disappearance of his photo from her drawing-room mantelpiece . . . .

Here is another incident equally typical of him. A well-known politician was being fairly generally abused, when without the slightest warning Kipling took up the cudgels in his behalf. He spoke in support of the fellow with such fiery sincerity, such generous warmth, that we all instantly assumed he was a close personal friend. Glossing over the more obvious flaws in the politician's character, he dwelt with amazing eloquence upon certain redeeming features of which we had no knowledge, and before he had finished those who had led the attack were thoroughly ashamed of themselves.

It so happened that I met this same M.P. a week or two later on a committee, and I couldn't resist telling him that he had a wonderful champion in Rudyard Kipling.

" Kipling ? " he said incredulously.

" Yes," I continued, " he's a tremendous admirer of yours—or is it that you are great friends ? "

" We haven't spoken to one another for years," came the astounding reply ; " in fact I think you might even describe us as deadly enemies."

Kipling has a passion for privacy that is almost comical. A man who had several times met him, and whose conversation he had apparently enjoyed, saw the famous imperialist airing himself in one of the Paris boulevards. Crossing over, he stood in front of him and held out his hand, saying as he did so :

" How do you do, Mr. Kipling ? "

The latter looked at the hand, looked at the man's face, looked at his boots. Then he said :

" I'm afraid you are mistaken. My name's Smith " —and passed on. . . . .

I have never known his equal at story-telling viva voce. Once he held a room spell-bound with his version of a yarn known to everyone who visits Quetta. In case any of my readers are unacquainted with it, I will condense it for their benefit.

There was a Colonel in command of the troops at Quetta who had just married a young and beautiful wife. They were devoted to one another and one thing only marred the happy prospect of their joint existence. This was the unspeakable terror his wife suffered whenever she saw a snake. As he was likely to be stationed in India for the remainder of his military career, it was a serious matter, and he resolved to cure her of what he was convinced was a mere nervous fancy.

One day he was out riding and a cobra crossed his path. His servants killed it—and then a thought struck him. He ordered them to hide it under something and bring it back to headquarters.

That night, when his wife had finished dressing for dinner and had gone downstairs, he put the dead snake on her bed and followed her.

After dinner he told his wife he had brought back something that afternoon which he hoped would be a pleasant surprise and which she would find on her bed upstairs. Up she went and the Colonel sat smoking awaiting developments.

Presently a loud scream came from the bedroom. The Colonel smiled and smoked on. Then he heard her call him by name. He smiled again and settled himself comfortably in his chair. Then there was a long silence. . . .

It was broken by the arrival of a servant who, almost choking with fear, informed him that the " memsahib " was lying dead on the floor of her bedroom.

" Nonsense ! " said the Colonel. " She has only fainted from fright. When she recovers she'll be cured of her fears."

But he went upstairs all the same.

The servant was right. His wife was dead in very truth. But not from fright. The cobra's mate had followed it to the house and must have been on the bed when the " memsahib " stopped to inspect her husband's " surprise." Two tiny punctures in the flesh of the Colonel's wife told their own story. . . .

Kipling gave us his interpretation of this painful incident with a wealth of vivid and realistic detail. A born master of dramatic narrative, he made the story live with a hundred additional touches which his pen alone could recapture.

When he had spoken the last word I heard a big intake of breath from his listeners, which was a greater tribute to his powers than all the applause that followed it. Then came the deluge. Fifteen people spoke at once, while the teller of tales sat tight and gazed hard into space with his mouth shut.

Questions by the score were bawled at him, but not a flicker of response appeared on his face. He seemed to have forgotten all about it. So the others went on talking to no one in particular until they had exhausted all they wanted to say.

When silence was completely restored, Kipling remarked prosaically : " The Colonel was a splendid fellow "—and changed the subject. . . .

§6

I had my first talk with Mark Twain at a dinner-party at the Savoy, and was immediately struck by the readiness of his wit. He did not, as so many clever men do, pause before a repartee. It left his tongue almost as soon as the other person had finished speaking.

Of course a great deal of conversational wit doesn't bear repetition; so much of its value lies in the atmosphere of the moment and the character or verbal peculiarity of its author; and this was especially true of Mark Twain's. He had a humorous personality which imparted humour to much that he said.

Once I read some of his flashes from my diary to a few intelligent friends, but as they only laughed politely I assumed it was the memory of Mark's manner that still kept them alive for me. I shall not, therefore, risk repeating them here.

But there was one aspect of his character I would like to illustrate. He hated fads and faddists and never tired of pouring ridicule upon them. His ridicule, however, was of the most subtle order. He never delivered a frontal attack. He drew his enemy on and on, and then, when his retreat was hopelessly cut off, proceeded to make mincemeat of him. I can record a priceless instance of this.

He was toying with a well-known vegetarian and agreeing absolutely with the theory that it was

horrible to live on the suffering of the brute creation.
He even got the vegetarian to agree that it was
horrible to live on the suffering of anything, and
that it was monstrous in us to assume—as the vivi-
sectionists did—that any form of life was less capable
of suffering than we ourselves. Then Mark got to
work.

"I can see," said he, "that you are absolutely at
one with me. We hate cruelty in any form. But
we are alas! ahead of our time."

Turning to the rest of the company, he proceeded
as follows:

"You should really try to see our point of view.
Cruelty in any form is obnoxious to us. We would
neither harm a fly nor pick a flower. Don't run
away with the idea that we are mere modern eccentrics. There have been souls similar to ours before.
Akbar, the great Mogul, once said that men do wrong
in making their stomachs the graves of animals.
But there he stopped. The higher humanitarianism
had not touched him. Why did he draw the line
at animals? By what right do we assume that a
rabbit is more sensitive to pain than a turnip? You
may reply that a rabbit squeals when it is hurt. But
that is merely because it was created with the organs
necessary to vocal expression. Dumb animals, in
fact, are anything but dumb. Besides, you are bound
to admit that even among ourselves there are degrees
of sensitivity as well as expressiveness. One man
can stand the extraction of three four-fanged teeth

without a murmur ; another will writhe the moment he sinks into the dentist's chair and howl when a finger is pressed against his gums. We must, I think, wholly discountenance the idea that because a hurt animal makes a noise, it is therefore subject to greater pain than a quiet vegetable."

At this point the vegetarian tried to interpose and had got as far as a " Look here ! " when Mark's passionate sympathy with oppressed parsnips broke out in an agony-stricken sentence :

" Have you," he urged, almost with tears in his eyes, " have you ever wrenched the heart out of a lettuce ? "

The other was too overcome to do more than shake his head, and Mark proceeded :

" If so, you will agree with me that the sound it makes is not wholly accounted for by friction. Many vegetables, like lobsters, change colour when they are cooked. Some wither when they are cut. Does that suggest a lack of feeling ? Several have various methods of signifying their hatred of human interference with their growth. In the case of the onion this method is lachrymal ; with others it is odoriferous or prickly.

" To me the truly degrading part of the whole wretched business is that we are not content with placing our consciences into the pot and leaving the fire to do the rest. We are persistently and callously vindictive. Only think of the millions who daily indulge in such hideous cruelty as gouging the eyes out of potatoes, flaying rhubarb, disembowelling pea-pods—to say nothing of such ghastly and refined torture as the quartering of French beans."

Some of the company were now so shaken with emotion that they had their handkerchiefs out, and the vegetarian saw that his last chance had come. Taking advantage of a pause, during which Mark wiped an eye, he cleared his throat and began : " Of course, Mr. Twain, I realize——"; but Mr. Twain was not to be caught in an argument before his peroration. He held up his hand authoritatively, blew his nose vigorously, and continued :

" Naturally, my dear friend, naturally. A man of your fine feeling and intelligence *must* realize that though the vegetable world is relatively mute and its only effective protest is by means of drug or poison (which, by the way, is far more frequently utilized than we are aware of), there is no proof whatever that its nervous system is not quite as highly developed as ours. And it is one of the most tragic facts in modern civilization that certain unimaginative vege-tarians, in their grave anxiety to spare partridges, are thoughtlessly brutal when they strip potatoes. Mr. Bernard Shaw has said that the idea of feeding on scorched corpses is horrible. He is quite right. I shudder to think of my early orgies, in which a prominent part was invariably played by the blood-red slabs of broiled beetroot. . . ."

Everybody was by this time in a state of collapse. The vegetarian simply vanished. Mark's face retained its gravity, and when the laughter had subsided he concluded with a twinkle in his eye:

" D'you know, there's a great deal in what I said. I might have converted myself but for the thought that a diet of oxygen would almost certainly upset my stomach."

CHAPTER IX

THE CRISIS

Lord Reading, Mr. Lloyd George, Mr. Asquith, Mr. Walter Cunliffe, Sir Edward Holden.

TO an intelligent observer the most noteworthy effect of the Great War has been the practically unlimited power vested in the big banking combines of Europe and America. The war gave the financiers their tremendous chance. They took it. And now more than ever before the bankers and financiers, not the politicians, are our rulers.

One cannot blame the bankers and financiers. In an individualist society such as ours the individual is encouraged to pursue a policy of power-grabbing, and he knows perfectly well that if he doesn't hold the reins someone else will. Of course it is generally realized that for centuries the real power behind the throne throughout Christendom has been the power of the givers (more often the withholders !) of credit. But their rise to absolute and naked supremacy began in August, 1914.

We had then, in England, a Chancellor of the

Exchequer whose almost incredible ignorance of finance can best be illustrated by the following story. When Mr. Lloyd George (for it was he) became Chancellor he asked the bankers to meet him, and this is what he said to them: "Well, gentlemen, it is my intention that British Credit shall be stronger than ever after my term of office. It shall stand at five per cent."

Sir Edward Holden tried to cover up what was surely a momentary lapse with a cough, and whispered to him: "But it already stands at two and a half per cent."

"Quite so," said Mr. Lloyd George, blithely unaware of the "howler" he was committing, "that is why I say it is my firm intention to make it stand at five per cent." Which indicated how suitable a man he was to have charge of the finances of the nation!

With men like this at the head of affairs, it is hardly to be wondered at that the bankers were able to stampede the politicians into panic-measures during the first week of August, 1914. There were hurried meetings at the Bank of England, flurried meetings at the Treasury. To his utter consternation the Chancellor learned that the volume of credit redeemable in gold on demand at that moment was more than twenty-five times the amount of gold the combined banks could scrape together. He was also horrified to hear that the instant the Balkan trouble started all the holders of cheques, bills, promissory

notes and other forms of credit, had taken the financial
authorities at their word and demanded gold—and
that the banks were unable to find five per cent of
the amount they owed.

The moment this " wizard of finance " grasped the
paralyzing fact that the banks were insolvent, and
that the whole banking system would unquestionably
break down under the stress of the crisis, he declared
a moratorium, said " hands off the banks," and issued
£1 and 10s. notes as legal tender—thus exchanging
these tokens of real credit for the bank credit, which
was even then exposed as worthless, and in the
process handing over the national credit to the
bankers.

One of the most momentous discussions in the
history of this country—charged with significance for
the future of our race—took place on the Saturday
night and Sunday morning of August 1st and 2nd,
1914. It was then that these far-reaching decisions
were made. Its scene was 11, Downing Street and
its principal actors were Mr. Lloyd George, Lord
Reading, Mr. Walter Cunliffe (Governor of the Bank
of England) and Sir Edward Holden (Chairman of
the London City and Midland Bank). There were
two others present, from one of whom I received
the report of what follows. It can be taken, with
allowances for slight verbal omissions or inaccuracies,
as an authoritative record of an incident hitherto
concealed from the public. It is not by any means
the whole discussion of those hectic hours. Many

other technical matters were gone into. But the extract here printed contains all that can be described as politically and humanly important.

After giving a brief résumé of that day's eventful happenings in the banking world, and stating that the Bank Rate had been advanced to ten per cent and that business was at a standstill, Cunliffe finished up with :

" So that's how the matter stands. Every bank in the country, including the Bank of England, will have to close its doors."

There was a long and fateful silence, broken at last by Mr. Lloyd George.

" The first thing to do," said he, " is to keep people quiet. It's no good pretending we know what to do. We don't. But we mustn't let them suspect it. . . . Unless we do something to prevent it, every bank, including the Post Office Savings Bank, will be besieged on Tuesday."

The remainder of the scene can be more conveniently set out thus :

READING : Yes, that must not be allowed. I suggest
    that you extend the Bank Holiday over Tuesday.
LL. G. : That's an idea ! Why not for the whole
    week ?
READING : I don't think so. You mustn't forget
    pay-day. We've got to have a plan by Thursday
    which can be put into operation on Friday.
    Otherwise you'll have something worse than a
    panic—you'll have riots. Extend the Bank

Holiday to Thursday — what d'you say, Cunliffe ?

CUNFLIFFE : That will certainly give us time. But it still doesn't give us a plan.

READING : The question we have to answer is this : How, in four days, are we going to make the people unlearn what they've been taught for at least a century ?

LL. G. : What's that ?

READING : Merely that all credit instruments are redeemable on demand in gold—eh, Cunliffe ?

CUNLIFFE : But they are.

READING : Indeed ? Then there is no crisis ?

CUNLIFFE : The position is abnormal. You can't say that we have failed because the financial system of the whole world is paralyzed. Our foreign balances are more than adequate to cover all our liabilities.

READING : The trouble is that they are foreign, isn't it ? And your depositors are in the mood to endorse the sentiment that charity begins at home.

LL. G. : Really, Rufus, I don't know what you're talking about—all this theorizing and so on. I mean, can't we *do* something ? Tell me what the public has got to be told and I'll see that it's served up all right. Northcliffe will help me with that.

READING : Then I repeat that first of all we've got to make the public realize they can't have gold, and secondly we've got to find the substitute.

Ll. G.: Well, the first's easy. It's unpatriotic. They've not only not got to ask for it, but they must give up what they've got.

Cunliffe: (*gloomily*) Yes, yes. If we can get them to bring in all the gold that's been hoarded and hand over their plate, etc., in exchange for notes, that would be a help. But so much of our reserve coin and bullion has gone abroad. I'm afraid that without the suspension of the Bank Act we can do nothing.

Holden: (*who has been quietly thinking*) It's obvious to me what we've got to do.

Ll. G.: Then why on earth didn't you say so before?

Holden: Because it has only just become obvious to me. . . . You'd better call a meeting, Cunliffe, at your place on Monday, and we'll adopt Reading's suggestion—extend the Bank Holiday over Thursday. And you (*pointing to Ll. G.*) will have to do what Goschen advised years ago—issue £1 and 10s. notes as legal tender.

Cunliffe: What?

Holden: Have you any other plan?

Cunliffe: N-n-no, but . . . .

Holden: Oh, I see what you're anxious about, but it need not necessarily be to our disadvantage.

Cunliffe: I don't see how it can fail to be.

Holden: If we can get the public to accept these

Treasury Notes instead of gold—and, after all, we know well enough that they will be as good as gold—we will get a new credit basis.

CUNLIFFE : Yes, but how are they going to be issued ? I can't see us getting much support at the meeting if the proposal is that the Government should set up a banking department.

HOLDEN : Obviously such a proposal wouldn't come from me.

LL. G. : Nor from me, gentlemen. You may rely on me not to do anything that would, by prejudicing banking interests, make matters more difficult at this difficult time.

READING : (*ironically*) Quite apart from making things more difficult at some future time.

LL. G. : (*after an awkward pause*) If you'll explain your plan a little more clearly, Sir Edward— my experience being more in the direction of collecting than issuing purchasing power—I will endeavour to assimilate what you have to say and be ready with whatever speeches it may be necessary for me to make in the next few days.

HOLDEN : I'm afraid I can't go into details now ; but roughly my proposal is that as it is essential to the safety of the nation that the banking system should not break down, you should support the banks by issuing these notes up to a certain proportion of their liabilities—this proportion to be discussed at the meeting which the Governor of the Bank of England will call for Monday. These Treasury Notes will be available for the payment of wages and will also form an adequate basis for the issue of fresh credits, which would otherwise be restricted by the dwindling reserves of gold held by the Bank of England. You should also suspend the Bank Act of '44 and permit the issue of notes beyond the statutory limit backed by a gold reserve. I think you'll find that will save the situation.

CUNLIFFE: And how do you propose to get rid of these Treasury Notes afterwards?

HOLDEN: You will never get rid of them. You must make up your mind as to that.

CUNLIFFE: They should have a gold backing.

HOLDEN: Not much use talking about a gold backing for them now, is there? What we've got to do at the moment is to get out of an almost desperate situation.

CUNLIFFE: I suppose you're right, but I don't like it a bit. I can see these powers in the hands of an unscrupulous Government—say a Socialist Government—being used wrongly to damage the financial system and possibly to destroy the credit of the country.

READING: I have not myself so high an opinion of the socialists' intelligence.

LL. G.: Then if I prepare a speech telling them that these notes are as good as gold and that the Government has saved the bankers——

CUNLIFFE : Oh, you mustn't do that ! That would be fatal.

HOLDEN : No, I hardly think it would be wise to suggest that the banks need saving.

READING : Of course not. Blame for the situation must be laid at the door of our foreign creditors.

LL. G. : Ah, well, that's easy enough. That appeals to me. It'll go down. But I suppose I can say that the Government is behind these notes ?

HOLDEN : Certainly. It is—isn't it ?

LL. G. : We have weathered so many storms that it is inconceivable we should be unable to weather this one. After all, the nation's credit was never more sound. (*Suddenly*) How many shall we print ?

HOLDEN : Can't tell you now. It's a question for Monday's meeting. Ten million as a start-off, I should say.

CUNLIFFE : There's one thing you've overlooked. How about bills falling due ? And how are we to deal with commercial paper generally ?

READING : I have been considering that. A moratorium will have to be declared.

LL. G. : A moratorium ?

READING : Yes—the desideratum of debtors, the curse of creditors.

At this point Mr. Asquith entered quietly and took a seat at the table. He nodded gravely to everyone present and broke the silence with a "Well?" addressed to the Chancellor.

LL. G. : These gentlemen think it will be necessary to declare a moratorium.

ASQUITH : For how long ?

CUNLIFFE : Let us have a month to start with. We may want longer.

ASQUITH : What ? A month ? It's unheard of !

READING : My dear Asquith, we have no precedent to go on in this case.

LL. G. : (*arrogantly*) And in any case we must not be ruled by precedent.

ASQUITH : (*ruminatively*) Yes, I suppose it's a case of desperate diseases requiring desperate remedies.

HOLDEN : Exactly.

ASQUITH : And what other measures do you propose, gentlemen ?

HOLDEN : I have been——

LL. G. : (*interrupting firmly*) It is proposed that we should extend the Bank Holiday over Thursday, and that during the first four days of the week we should utilize every minute to inspire the public with confidence. Further, that by an issue of £1 and 10s. notes from the Treasury we should stop the demand for gold and yet enable wages to be paid and the business of the country to be carried on.

ASQUITH : You mean that the proposal is to inflate the currency ?

LL. G. : Well—er——

HOLDEN : Precisely. It is the only thing to do.

ASQUITH : And your safeguard, Sir Edward?

HOLDEN : The ill-effects, if any, will not be noticeable at first, and I myself doubt very much if there will be any ill-effects at all.

CUNLIFFE : I can hardly help viewing the step with grave misgivings.

LL. G. : We must all be prepared to take risks.

READING : (*yawning*) Well, who's for bed?

ASQUITH : No bed for me, I fear. It looks as though I shall have an all-night session with Grey. . . .

Shortly afterwards the meeting broke up, though Mr. Lloyd George took a turn with Sir Edward Holden in St. James's Park before retiring for the night.

CHAPTER X

STATESMEN AT HOME

1. *Mr. Asquith, Mr. Lloyd George, Mr. Winston Churchill, Sir Edward Grey.*

2. *Lord Curzon, Mr. Arthur Balfour, Lord Robert Cecil.*

DURING the war I was in constant communication with all the chief ministers of the Crown. My time was spent partly in Paris, partly in Washington, partly in Rome, but chiefly in London. I got to know, in some cases intimately, men whom I had previously had dealings with only by letter. I met them officially and unofficially, on committees and in cabarets, on duty and off duty.

With a very few exceptions I found them personally charming but politically deplorable. I mean that they were for the most part out for personal aggrandizement. It is a matter of grave social and historical importance that the people should know their rulers, should know the kind of men who govern them and the kind of men who preach to them. Without that knowledge they can never learn the lessons which, taught in time, might prevent unspeakable tragedy.

It is to help forward such knowledge that I have consented to the publication of certain parts of my diary. For I have seen these men at close quarters and can speak of them frankly and truthfully, careless of censure or praise. My book will, I hope, be a corrective to all the second-hand and second-rate personality-patter (as I call it) that has appeared since the war.

My diary is full of verbatim reports of official meetings and the talk at dinner-parties during the war period. It is difficult to pick a scene or two that will convey precisely that shade of con-scienceless egotism that I found wherever I went. However, I have done my best and the scenes that follow are typical of the rest.

I might of course have made two composite scenes out of many, in order the better to portray character, but upon reflection I have decided to publish two separate scenes exactly as they occurred. They are chosen with the object of presenting as many of the qualities of the participants as could be got into single episodes.

And here I would like to comment in advance upon the obvious criticism these scenes will call forth. It is frequently supposed by people who don't know any better that men in the limelight are differently constituted from men who are not. Like many other popular notions, this is a pure fallacy.

I have seen politicians, like the famous Lord Salisbury, talk to their colleagues in a manner that no scullery-maid could improve upon. We are all human, and a man only looks at his best when he is posing before the public.

Nevertheless the popular conception of famous men is a fixed and immovable one, and I shall not escape the charge of distortion. The bald truth is usually called a burlesque and the scenes that follow will be described as too good to be true—except by the cognoscenti, who will know that they are too good *not* to be true. Gradually I am coming to the belief that life cannot be burlesqued. Things I have seen done and heard said would put the wildest fiction to shame ; and I cannot too emphatically state what is to me a platitude—namely, that certain quite normal people and certain phases of quite normal life out-caricature their most outrageous caricatures. " Incredible ! " will spring to the lips of the uninstructed. Well, it is my business to instruct them.

What follows, then, is as true as a first-class memory and a proved faculty for the reconstruction of incident and dialogue can make it. Both episodes were entered up in my diary, word for word as they appear here, within a few hours of their occurrence. It is my hope that they will help some future historian to understand the motives and characters of certain British politicians at a serious juncture in our history. They may also help him to explain to his readers why we took so long to win the war—though he will have to hunt for similar scenes between German politicians if he has to explain why we won it at all!

§1

One evening in the early part of the year 1916 I was dining at 10, Downing Street. There were not more than twelve of us all told and the conversation was tinged with the gloom of the latest casualty lists. The Prime Minister, Mr. Asquith, was doing his best to keep the ball of talk rolling, but there were moments when he seemed preoccupied and restless.

The departure of the ladies to the drawing-room upstairs was, it must be confessed, a relief, and the instant the door closed behind them we settled down comfortably to the topic that was uppermost in everyone's mind. Two or three of us began to speak at once, only stopping when Asquith's voice boomed through the cloud of cigar smoke in which he had enveloped himself:

"I am expecting great news to-night," he said.

Upon which Lloyd George remarked:

"You always are, but it never comes."

A faint " Ssh ! " came from Sir Edward Grey.

" Haig is confident," continued Asquith, " that things are moving at last."

" Probably they are," from the irrepressible Lloyd George—"backwards ! "

Winston Churchill, who was sitting close to the last speaker, nudged him warningly and said something I couldn't quite catch, something that sounded like : " Let us hear what he has to say."

" Backwards perhaps," Asquith went on, " but that is merely the crouch before the spring."

In spite of another " Ssh ! " from Sir Edward Grey and another nudge from Churchill, Lloyd George burst out peevishly :

" I don't believe it. We'll never do anything until we make up our minds. The nation must be roused to a sense of its danger. People think we are winning because we've got Kitchener. I think we're losing because we've got Kitchener. Wherever one goes, it's Kitchener this, Kitchener that, Kitchener the other thing. Nothing but Kitchener ! "

There was a pause while Asquith carefully helped himself to a glass of port. Then, very slowly, he said :

" You speak bitterly. Are you jealous of Kitchener ? "

The other expressed his contempt for such an idea with a noise that sounded like " Pfff ! "

" For my part," continued Asquith, " I think Kitchener a big man——"

" Six feet, two and a half inches," came the ready retort.

" And," pursued the Prime Minister taking no notice of the interruption, " what is more to the point just now, the right man . . . . Fill your glass, Winston. . . . Without him, say what you will, we would never have had an army worth the name.

He is a great patriot, too. He has no petty ambitions to gratify, no personal vanity, no jealousy. Not one of us sitting here would have remained in office for a week if it hadn't been for him."

" Oh, come ! " exclaimed Churchill, " that's rather strong. How d'you make that out ? "

" Whenever there's a war," answered our host, " the country turns instinctively to the Conservative Party. We gave them Kitchener, and saved our own skins by doing so."

" And who, pray, suggested him for the job ? " asked Lloyd George with a hint of triumph in his manner.

" The idea first came from Northcliffe," returned the P.M.

" Ah ! " The note of triumph was more insistent.

" Why do you say that ? " queried Asquith.

" Northcliffe now thinks him a back-number." With these words Lloyd George sat back in his chair, crossed his legs, and looked up at the ceiling.

" Which is simply another way of saying that Northcliffe wants to run another man," retaliated the harassed leader.

" What's his latest little game ? " interposed Churchill.

" Ask David," said Asquith—and a titter of laughter greeted the sally.

Lloyd George leant across the table and with some emphasis begged to know what the Prime Minister was getting at.

"Nothing, my dear fellow, nothing at all," came the dulcet response; "except that you're Northcliffe's latest catch, so it was natural to assume you had risen to his bait."

"I know nothing whatever of catches or baits," was the angry answer. "All I know is that Northcliffe's fed-up with Kitchener."

"Did he tell you so?"

"That's an insidious question and I refuse to answer it."

"Well, well, what does it matter? Let us leave it at that."

Lloyd George was on the point of retorting when Grey intercepted quickly:

"What's the alternative suggestion?"

Asquith smiled, sipped his port, and then replied: "Ask David."

There was another laugh from the rest of us, broken into by Lloyd George, who slapped the table, jumped from his seat, and marched over to the fireplace, with the words:

"If you say that again, Asquith, I shall lose my temper."

He might have gone on, but at this moment there was a knock at the door and a secretary came in to tell the Premier he was wanted on the telephone. Asquith excused himself and hurried out. During his absence the conversation continued in this strain:

CHURCHILL: I wish you two wouldn't always quarrel.

Ll. G. : I never quarrel.

Churchill : Well, I wish you wouldn't allow others to quarrel with you, if you'd rather I put it that way.

Ll. G. : Asquith's getting impossible; he becomes more querulous and conservative every day——

Grey : Really, I can hardly——

Ll. G. : Oh, I know you're devoted to him and feel you ought to stick up for him. But it's no good. He hangs on to his friends because they *are* his friends and lets the country go to the devil! The situation is ridiculous. Europe is laughing at us. In self-defence I shall have to resign.

Churchill : My father used to say : " Never resign until you're indispensable."

Ll. G. : Yes, and a pretty fair mess of things *he* made, didn't he ?

Churchill : The theoretical truth of a maxim does not depend upon the failure or success of its practical application.

Ll. G. : Rather a laboured epigram, Winston, but better than Asquith's stifling platitudes.

Grey : I think the less said against the Prime Minister behind his back the better.

Ll. G. : I say nothing whatever against him—except that he can't look facts in the face, doesn't know black from white, distrusts his ablest lieutenants, would rather lose the war than not behave like a gentleman, and thinks he knows everything because he was at Oxford.

At this point Churchill laughed outright, while Sir Edward Grey, myself and a diplomatic colleague experienced considerable difficulty in keeping our faces. Churchill handed the cigars to Lloyd George, who, after taking and lighting one, summed up his feelings in the phrase : " I'm sick to death of all this damned shilly-shallying."

" Is seems to me," said Churchill, " that you're sick to death of everything."

" Don't be childish ! " snapped the other. " Where's the port ? Oh, thanks."

" Would you like to take the job on ? " Churchill put in quietly as he knocked the ash off his cigar.

" Of course I would ! " cried Lloyd George without a second's hesitation. Then, suddenly realizing what he had said, he pulled himself up and asked Churchill what job he was referring to.

" The Premiership," said the latter, still giving his attention to the cigar.

" Oh, that ! "

" Why, what did you think I meant ? "

" I don't know. When you spoke I was thinking of something else."

We all looked at one another but nobody spoke. A somewhat heavy silence ensued, interrupted at last by the return of Asquith. Still no one spoke. Eventually Sir Edward Grey asked if he had received any news. Asquith nodded his head and murmured

" Bad." Pressed as to its nature, he admitted that there had been another set-back on the Western Front. Thereafter the talk went briskly forward:

LL. G.: I told you it would be a move in that direction.

ASQUITH: Quite so.

LL. G.: We must have Kitchener up and tackle him.

ASQUITH: Why?

LL. G.: There's bungling somewhere, and he's sitting on it like a sphinx. He should be asked to resign.

ASQUITH: This is the second time you've wanted to get rid of him. If it hadn't been for me he would never have returned from the Dardanelles.

LL. G.: Pity he ever did! We must find some excuse to send him to another front.

CHURCHILL: Not the Western, for heaven's sake, or you'll have more squalls from Paris and squeals from G.H.Q.

ASQUITH: I'm agreeable that he should be asked to make a statement. I've been approached about it already. And I'm sure he'd be the first to acquiesce.

LL. G.: (*sarcastically*) Very handsome of him indeed!

ASQUITH: But we can't send him out of the country again. He's too popular. Even Northcliffe came a crash when he attacked him. Besides,

we must treat him honourably and generously.
He deserves well of us.

Ll. G. : If *you* don't do something, it'll be done in
spite of you.

Asquith : In that case I may leave Downing Street,
but I shall take my honour with me.
(*Lloyd George, still at the fire-place, was heard to
say something that sounded perilously like " Stuff ! "*)

Asquith : (*markedly changing the conversation*) I have
been reading Dickens lately, and——

Ll. G. : (*explosively*) Oh, damn Dickens !

Asquith : Really, my dear sir, you might have the
kindness to let me finish my sentence.

Ll. G. : (*with a gesture of resignation*) All right ; fire
away ! But whatever you do, don't hit the
enemy.

Asquith : (*after a pause*) I repeat that I have been
reading Dickens lately, and I am astonished to
find him so little behind the times. There are
two first-class portraits of Northcliffe in " Our
Mutual Friend." They are so life-like that if
one didn't know Northcliffe to be an illiterate
sensation-monger, one might almost suppose he
had modelled himself on Podsnap and Veneering.

Grey : But is he illiterate ?

Asquith : Ask David.

Ll. G. : (*furiously*) Look here, Asquith——

Grey : Please, *please* !

Churchill : I'm not exactly a man of peace myself,
but I really think . . . .

Ll. G. : (*fiercely*) Sorry. You were saying, Asquith ?

Asquith : I was saying . . . . Circulate the port,
Winston. Thanks . . . . I was saying . . . . By
the way, what *was* I saying ? . . . . Oh, yes !
I remember . . . . But I hardly think we can gain
much by pursuing these topics.

The conversation now became more general, and,
to everyone's relief, more trivial. About ten minutes
later, Asquith suggested that we should join the
ladies. By this time the atmosphere had cleared
and Lloyd George was chatting and laughing with
much affability.

§2

The second episode I have selected took place a
year later. Lord Curzon, Lord Robert Cecil and
myself were dining in Carlton House Terrace with
Mr. Arthur Balfour. It was early in 1917, and by
the time we had reached the stage of coffee and
liqueurs an air-raid had begun in the remoter suburbs
of London.

Neither Balfour nor Curzon showed the slightest
consciousness of the distant gun-fire and bomb-
dropping, though both were quite audible. Cecil
and I, on the other hand, were acutely conscious of
it and kept pricking up our ears whenever a particularly resonant crash came through the persistent
mutter and murmur of hostilities.

The conversation drifted from the fugues of Bach
to the paradoxes of G. K. Chesterton, and from the

moment we sat down to dinner to the moment we got up it would be true to say that the spirit of the period did not in any shape or form penetrate the walls of that room. The atmosphere throughout was—well, I can only describe it as eighteenth century. True, the subjects discussed were mostly topical, but the manner of discussion and the " temper " of the chief talkers (Curzon and Balfour) were distinctly pre-Revolution and pre-Romantic.

I cannot do better than set down the dialogue that began with the coffee and the first dull thumping of the air-raid in the form I have elsewhere adopted :

MYSELF : (*trying to swing the conversation round to the war*) Has anyone seen Bottomley's latest ?

CECIL : No.

CURZON : Hardly.

BALFOUR : I'm afraid——

CECIL : Never read anything of his. What does he write about ?

CURZON : God and politics—chiefly God.

BALFOUR : It would be amusing to picture Bottomley's God. Mind, he's the God of the whole British race. That is where St. Horatio is so clever. He says the silly things that the majority of the mob would like to say if only they were without a sense of shame—that is, if they hadn't a sense of humour.

CECIL : He appears to be exercising a terrible influence just now—an influence wholly for bad, I'm afraid.

BALFOUR : Oh, don't say that ! He is, perhaps, our greatest comic writer. In a sense I owe more to him than to anyone alive. Never, in my most dejected moments, has the thought of him and his inimitable writings failed to cheer me up. He is my great war-time relaxation—better for the mind than a game of golf for the body. There are moments when I feel the world would be utterly unendurable without him. Times without number, when "Punch" and even the Labour papers have been unable to alleviate my depressed spirits, Mr. Bottomley's leading articles have brought balm to my soul.

CURZON : (*laughing*) Good ! Excellent ! I couldn't beat it myself. Go on, Arthur.

BALFOUR : Now wherein lies the secret of his inspiration ? Dare we pry into the recesses of that big human soul of his ? Can we, in short, get to the bottom of Mr. Bottomley ? I fear not. There is a miraculous element about all great teachers and comedians that cannot, indeed *must* not, be explained away.

MYSELF : Have you often heard him speak ?

BALFOUR : Quite frequently I have had that unspeakable privilege. The perorations of our heaven-born publicist have sometimes had such an effect upon me that more than once I have had to be helped from the House on to the terrace outside, where I have lain prostrate for several minutes, slowly recovering from severe, if necessary, attacks of lung-suppression.

CURZON: Ha, ha! Splendid! You are wasting your time in the fields of philosophy. You should turn your hand to satire.

BALFOUR: I think not. All these great public heroes satirize themselves far better than I could do it for them.

CURZON: A true biography of Bottomley would be an invaluable book. In it we could trace the decline and fall of civilization since the introduction of cheap journalism.

BALFOUR: Yes, that is certainly an idea. Perhaps I should write to " John Bull " about it. . . . But no! That would never do. Though I may dream of immortalizing Mr. Bottomley, I couldn't possibly dream of bothering Mr. Bottomley. For I firmly believe that the few moments he is able to snatch from his active and totally disinterested efforts on behalf of great human and humorous causes are spent meekly upon his knees—and who am I that I should bid him rise ? (*General laughter.*)

CECIL: You are a facetious beggar, Arthur. But let us, if you don't mind, turn to more serious matters. When are you off to America ?

BALFOUR: In a few weeks.

CECIL: What do you expect to do there ?

BALFOUR: Raise the temperature, my dear fellow.

CECIL: How ?

BALFOUR : By means of my benign and ingratiating manner. There is nothing the Americans love so much as a real blue-blood aristocrat. If my kid gloves cannot inspire the mailed fist, nothing can. All the New York papers have been provided with the necessary " dope " (as I believe they call it). I am to be acclaimed as the Heir of All the Ages, the Scion of Eliza's Spacious Days, *et hoc genus omne.* It will be a most interesting experience. The idea originated with Lloyd George. He has a flair for this kind of thing. His own pulse is so exquisitely attuned to the vibrations of the populace that an effective plebeian gesture comes as easily to him as reading Benedetto Croce does to me.

CURZON : Curious—is it not ?—that we should have lived to see that fellow cock-of-the-walk. I remember a time when King Edward refused to have him at a garden party and Salisbury used to call him " The whipper-snapper."

BALFOUR : The world revolves, my dear George, in spite of us. I, too, remember a time when you used to write poetry. By the way, are you still turning out verse ?

CURZON : Once a poet, always a poet.

BALFOUR : Indeed ? But I thought someone had invented a cure.

CURZON : Oh, yes ! A cure was invented years ago.

BALFOUR : Really ? What was it ?

CURZON : The Laureateship.

MYSELF : (*laughing*) Poetry belongs to one's youth.
Age turns to prose.

CURZON : Hardly that, I think. Poetry is the expression of *rebellious* youth only. That is why
a romance that begins with a sonnet usually
ends in the divorce court.

CECIL : I shouldn't have thought you were ever a
rebel.

BALFOUR : George has always rebelled against
rebellion.

CURZON : Tell me : are you going to lecture the
Americans for not coming into the war until
they saw there were no more dollars to be made
out of it ?

BALFOUR : No, I shall listen politely while the
Americans lecture me on the ease with which
the war will be won now that they *have* come
into it.

CECIL : Do all Americans lecture ?

BALFOUR : Nearly all, I am told.

CURZON : And those who don't, listen to those who
do. It's a form of national sport—like football
in England.

BALFOUR : You see, they take life very seriously over
there. They never tire of learning something
new, and they are not ashamed of passing on
what they have learnt for the benefit of their
fellow-citizens. First they find out all they can
about everything, and then they mention it to
everyone they meet.

MYSELF : Every American a sort of walking information bureau, eh ?

BALFOUR : So I imagine. They are very up-to-date.

CURZON : Except in their religion.

CECIL : Why in their religion ?

CURZON : Well, the ancient Egyptians worshipped cats, and the modern Americans are casting themselves at Pussy's foot.

(*General laughter.*)

CECIL : Ha, ha ! That's neat. You're in form to-night.

BALFOUR : At any rate there is one thing for which the rest of the world cannot be sufficiently grateful to the United States.

CECIL : What is that ?

BALFOUR : It has steadfastly declined to misgovern any country except its own.

CURZON : You are right. The trouble with the world at present is that people bother their heads about one another far too much. My experience is that very few people are capable of looking after their own affairs, let alone the affairs of a hundred million others.

BALFOUR : But there is great safety in numbers, George, and politicians can do less damage to an Empire than to a nation. A man who will wreck his own home is often quite harmless on a committee.

CECIL : Then what on earth is the use of parliament ?

BALFOUR : The real object of all parliaments is to give the democracy a feeling of security. Besides, the House of Commons keeps a lot of people out of mischief. Only think how terrible it would be if the folk who can talk to their lungs' content inside the House (after all, you and I can always retreat to the smoking-room) were let loose to bawl at us instead from every street-corner. It is bad enough at election-time as it is, but that fortunately only comes at rare intervals —when, in fact, the government in power has bored its own party to extinction.

CECIL : I wonder what your constituents would say if they heard you talking like that ?

BALFOUR : They would content themselves with gaping. The country will stand almost anything from men whose names are in everyone's mouth. (*He pauses to let the reverberations of some uncomfortably contiguous explosion die away.*) This is a terrible age. The Jew is coming into his own and the democrat follows obediently at his heels. The rise of democracy synchronizes with the renaissance of Jewry. And to think that Isaac's ancestors had his teeth pulled out by ours !

MYSELF : (*laughing*) King John seems to have had a fairly extensive practice among the forebears of our new rulers.

CURZON : Yes, they paid him enormous sums for gasless extractions.

BALFOUR : But what they lost in teeth during his reign, they gained in titles afterwards. (*Laughter.*)

MYSELF : (*making another effort to turn the talk into more serious channels*) The news from Russia is bad.

BALFOUR : I'm not in the least surprised——

All the time the noise of the air-raid had been gradually increasing, as the hostile aircraft penetrated the outer defences and streamed across the centre of the metropolis. At this particular point in the conversation a most terrific detonation filled the air. The whole building shook from its foundations. Several window-panes were shattered. The sound of tiles clattering on the pavement outside mingled with the thunder and roar of London's artillery and the boom and crash of the enemy's bombs. Mr. Balfour made the most of the interruption and sipped his liqueur. At the first comparative lull in the prevailing din, he continued from where he left off :

BALFOUR : A nation that can produce Dostoievski, Turgeniev and Gorki, to say nothing of Tchehov and Tolstoi, is capable of anything. (*Another earth-shaking explosion.*) The fount of all their art is not symmetry, but the cemetery.

CURZON : I have met a great number of Russians in my time. There was something lacking in all of them. Strange—isn't it ?—that so few Russian marriages turn out happy.

BALFOUR : They are not alone in that. Monogamy,

which exists as a mere economic necessity, has been tried and found wanting. In every country the large majority of so-called happy marriages are simply habit marriages. . . . You aren't drinking, George.

CURZON : I am thinking . . . . I wonder if what you say is really true ?

BALFOUR : Undoubtedly. But is that a reason why you shouldn't drink ? . . . . Ah, I see ! Abstinence makes the heart grow fonder.

CURZON : Do you speak from experience ?

BALFOUR : Yes—other people's.

CECIL : (*interrupting vigorously*) It really is the most extraordinary thing. For the last twenty minutes you two have been sitting there, talking about nothing in particular, and so far neither of you has deigned to remark the fact that the most unholy racket is going on outside. I'm very sorry, but I can't stand it any longer. It's getting on my nerves. I must go out and see what's happening.

BALFOUR : You shouldn't cultivate a conscience, Robert. I have often had to speak to you about it.

MYSELF : That last bomb couldn't have been much further than Piccadilly. I'm coming with you. (*Both rise.*)

BALFOUR : You won't mind if we continue our trivialities ?

MYSELF : Not in the least.

CECIL : Though how you can do so passes my comprehension.

(*Boom. Crash. Rattle.*)

BALFOUR : Take a cigar with you.

CECIL : It seems to me that we shall be fortunate if we take our lives with us.

BALFOUR : That is no argument against a " Corona."

CECIL : All right.

So we took a cigar each, gulped down our liqueurs and made for the door. I opened it and Lord Robert Cecil dashed across the hall. Just before closing the door behind me I heard Curzon say :

" We must have a little peace now and then—otherwise we'd never remember what we were fighting for."

To which Balfour made reply :

" All our wars are fought in order to find out which of our friends is our worst enemy. Besides—"

But I couldn't wait for any more. Shutting the door, I followed Lord Robert across the hall, down the stairs and into the street—leaving those two philosophers to their pleasant pre-war reveries. Perhaps it is my misfortune that I haven't an eighteenth century temperament during an air-raid. . . .

CHAPTER XI

OLLA PODRIDA

Lord Riddell, Horatio Bottomley, Father Bernard Vaughan, President Wilson, Georges Clemenceau, Ramsay Mac-Donald, Philip Snowden, Sidney Webb.

STREWN about my diary over a period of many years are references to people and events now forgotten. There are also not a few recorded incidents that, for the moment at any rate, had better remain where they are. But going through the pages I have garnered a few anecdotes here and there of persons and things that retain their interest for the present age and that can be published without causing too much uneasiness in the quarters most concerned.

These I have lumped together under the above chapter-heading; they form, as it were, a series of desultory foot-notes to some of the more purposeful pictures that precede them, and all of them help to illustrate those curious turns and twists of personality that enable the biographer to exhibit his full-length portrait. . . .

THE WHISPERING GALLERY

§1

As I began my picture-gallery with a famous news-paper proprietor, I cannot do better than begin this collection of snapshots, as I may call them, with another. His name: Lord Riddell.

I first met him in Washington. We all knew him as Lloyd George's chief henchman, a man who had spotted the little Welsh horse as a certain winner and had backed him for all he was worth. We also knew him as the owner of " The News of the World," a man who had a pretty cute understanding of the appeal of sensation to an illiterate public and had backed that " cert." also for all it was worth. He came amongst us, then, in the not very alluring light of the new plutocratic peerage. And I think I may say that he staggered the lot of us.

We expected to see something like a " bookie," but we saw something much more like a bookman. His face, his figure, above all his tastes and interests, emphatically contradicted the " boomster " and sensation-monger we knew him to be. It was obviously another case of Jekyll and Hyde.

I sometimes tried to picture the ascetic and scholarly face transformed by the trickery of his trade. How would he look in that Downing Street armchair when his wily master was explaining the messianic aspect of some exceptionally mundane " coup " they were cogitating together? How would he appear to his Fleet Street underlings when he was deciding how to make " The News of the World " still more newsy, not to say nosey ? But such picturings are profitless. I must confine myself to the man as he appeared to me.

Let me say at once that he gave me the clear impression of a scientist manqué. Had he not had to work for his living, his life would have been spent in a ceaseless search after facts. He has an appetite for figures that a professional mathematician would envy. He can pour out statistics by the hour—as he literally did at one dinner-party, from soup to savoury ! His manner no less than his matter is that of the donnish savant. He never raises or lowers his voice, which is nevertheless a masterful one. There is a calmness, a mansuetude, about his pose, his gestures, his intonations, his whole personality in fact, that make one rub one's eyes and wonder whether this can possibly be the man whose headlines howl from the hoardings of two hemispheres.

Sitting in a chair he usually rests his elbows on the arms, making a bridge with his hands just in front of his face and looking carefully with lowered head across the top of this bridge. It was in such a posture that he told a few of us late one evening the story of his first step to fortune. I was not feeling well that night and omitted to enter up my diary before going to bed, not finding time to do so until the following night. I say this to excuse the fact that I cannot give his story verbatim ; the actual words he used had slipped my memory in the interval and I could only record the bare outline.

I may mention here that my memory is astonishingly accurate, right down to the pauses in a conversation and the tone of a voice, for eight or even twelve hours. Which means that any entry in my diary dealing with the events of the day on which the entry was made can be absolutely relied upon. This of course was purely a matter of training. But whenever I neglected my diary for twenty-four hours, it was with difficulty that I could recall particulars and usually had to content myself with a general outline. This story of Lord Riddell's is therefore true in substance if not quite accurate in detail.

He started life as an underpaid clerk and spent his spare time in wandering about London gazing at bookshops and wishing he had money to buy some of the choice works within. One day he was sent on business to interview a client in some South London suburb. The client was not at home, so Riddell said he would wait. He was shown into the drawing-room, where he instantly became absorbed in contemplation of a " collected " edition of some classic author, one volume of which appeared to be missing. When the client arrived and they had discussed their business, Riddell pointed to the bookcase and remarked upon the missing volume.

"Yes," said the client, "I have spent pounds and pounds in searching for that volume. I'd give anything to be able to complete the edition, because the set is quite unobtainable now and of great value."

A few days later (no wonder Lord Riddell is a

great admirer of popular romance) he was standing
before a bookshop in the Strand, when—could it be ?
No, surely ! Yes, no doubt about it ! There, as
plain as a peerage, was the missing volume !

That same evening found him in Tooting, or
wherever it was, ringing the front-door bell of his
boss's client.

" How much did you say you would give for
that missing volume ? "

" Anything you like to mention."

" A thousand pounds ? "

" Don't be silly ! Anything within reason, I
mean."

" At what do you price ' reason ' ? "

" Have you found the volume ? "

" Oh, no ! "

" Then why waste my time ? "

" I just wanted to know—in case."

" I see. Well, I'd give £100 for that missing
volume."

" You mean that ? "

" I do."

" Thank you. Good-evening."

Riddell walked back to the Strand—those were his
early " Whittington " days and he couldn't afford a
'bus, though already Bow bells were calling to him,
" Turn again, Riddell, my Lord, Newspaper-Magnate "
—and entered the bookshop. With a steady voice
and a studied indifference of demeanour he asked the
price of the odd volume.

" Oh, you can have that for ninepence ! "

Here a visit to a neighbouring pawnshop, where he temporarily dispensed with his waistcoat, was advisable. The agony of those minutes, during which any stray caller might have picked up the volume and strolled off with it, effectually muffled the sound of Bow bells ; but they rang out in a deafening diapason as he marched out of the shop with the coveted tome under his arm.

One would have thought that Fate had already opened its treasure-box widely enough. But one would have thought wrongly. Our Pantomime Prince was not too overcome with emotion to inspect the article he had procured at the risk of catching his death of cold. And lo ! hidden furtively between two pages was the " Last Will and Testament " of a person unknown to the shivering youth.

As this did not appear to be an illustration of the text, and as it could hardly appeal to the bibliophile for whom he had obtained the work, our hero trans-ferred the manuscript from the pages to his pocket— and Bow bells were audible that evening all the way to Tooting.

We were not vouchsafed the remainder of this touching narrative. But I rather gathered that the " Will " no less than the volume helped him on his road to glory, and that in turning over the leaves of the latter he had " turned " to some purpose. . . .

My diary records two or three more meetings with Riddell and several amusing stories of public men which he told us—too intimate for present publication. Also a " mot " of his which is well worthy of a place here.

Talking of Lloyd George, one of us asked him whether he really thought the Prime Minister (as he then was) had done everything people credited him with off his own bat, whether in short he had set the Thames on fire. Riddell thought for a moment ; then answered in that even voice of his :

" Well, no ; perhaps he did not exactly set the Thames on fire, but he certainly ignited a pretty considerable bonfire in Parliament Square."

Riddell's story of how he negotiated the purchase of " The Daily Chronicle " for Lloyd George at a critical juncture in the latter's fortunes was another choice morsel I gleaned for the pleasure of posterity.

§2

Something that Lord Riddell said about Horatio Bottomley : " He is the chief thorn in our side, but he won't prick us much longer "—brings me to the second ingredient of my olla podrida.

Bottomley had the art possessed by few of making you feel that, for him, you were the only person in the world worth talking to ; also that there was nothing on earth you couldn't trust him with, from your secrets to your silver, and nothing on earth he wouldn't do for you. (As things turned out the last two words demand transposition.)

In many respects he was a very good man, kind-hearted, jovial, generous, and extremely sensitive to injustice. A tale of woe that couldn't for an instant have imposed upon his brain frequently wrung his heart ; and as nearly all his benefactions were called forth by the impulse of the moment, his name did not appear on charity subscription lists anything like as often as the names of those who condemned him.

His rise and fall—I mean the mere fact that either was possible—impeach the social system of his day, a system whereby thousands get rich at the expense of their fellows and by means every bit as questionable as those employed by him. But since they fleeced the community by legal sanction whereas he fleeced it by moral suasion, they continue to live in possession of their respectability while he is punished for daring to be in possession of a superior imagination. But I am not writing a tract for the times ; so, having gently addressed the jackal-publicists and moralists who couldn't even contain their hypocrisy when Bottomley went to Brixton, let us return to Horatio.

My acquaintanceship with him began in 1902, and though I have met and spoken with him on many occasions since, it is an incident in that early association that I wish to relate. In those days I was interested in the theatre, especially the poetic drama, and as I had a little money to speculate with, I was rather anxious to invest it in some theatrical enterprise. A friend introduced me to Bottomley, who then had a finger in several managerial pies, and he asked me to come and breakfast with him.

Breakfast with Bottomley! It is strange to look back upon it now. I really don't know what we didn't discuss. My diary mentions something like forty different topics, starting with frogs, which he insisted were an admirable early-morning dish, and ending with a dissertation on the " favourites " of the last few Derbys. His range of interests was truly remarkable, though his method of discourse was rather reminiscent of Mrs. Nickleby's. I pick a passage at random :

" Don't run away with the idea that the only drinkable white wines come from France. Spain provides some of the best ; but as France has the monopoly, the worst Spanish wines are shipped over to France, bottled there and exported as French. And talking of wines, help yourself to some coffee. More people come to ruin through strong coffee than you'd believe. . . . These kidneys are leathery. Would you like me to order some more ? All right. Try the kedjeree. That's Keir Hardie's favourite fodder. Says it makes his speeches spicey. So I told him to chuck eating it. He's a better man than most of them, all the same. You couldn't buy him as you could the rest—Burns and all. Rum cuss ! He once told me his sole reading was the Bible and the blue books. Funny mixture ! Great poetry in the Bible. Have you read it ? A lot of stuff in your line, too. I take my hat off to Moses as a diplomat."

All the time he was vigorously assaulting his kidneys and bacon and punctuating his comments with a somewhat noisy method of munching. It would take a Sherlock Holmes on the top of his form to trace the mental steps whereby, during a slight pause for mastication, he left Moses and arrived at a mummer :

" I don't think the old man's a paying proposition," he said.

" What old man ? " I asked.

" Henry Irving," he replied, lifting his eyebrows slightly to suggest that I evidently hadn't been following him. Another pause for another munch and he continued :

" Ever since Ellen Terry left him he's gone all to pieces. Never knew a man to be so dotty on a woman as he has been on her. Every word she uttered was God's law in his theatre. If she didn't like a thing, out it went. If she didn't like a man, out he went. He dropped all his old friends for her, and now that she's dropped him he's finished. Even his art has ceased to interest him. He's living on the echo of his former self, on the loyalty of a fast-dying public. Fine old fellow, in his way. But I shouldn't advise you to put your money on a horse that's gone groggy at the knees. Anyhow, here's Forbes-Robertson who wants a backer. I got him some money to produce ' Hamlet ' five years ago.

He's a nice fellow and a good ' spec.' Many worse, I promise you. . . . Try some of that honey; it's good tackle. Made by my own bees. Ever gone in for bees? Quaint customers. Wish I had more time to look after them. . . . Now it's your turn to do some talking."

There you have Bottomley in a nutshell. He was full of himself and his doings, full of information, full of other people and events. Bubbling over with vitality, cross-grained upon occasion, humorous, entertaining, interested in the manifold affairs of life. You couldn't bottle him up for long; he had to keep going. Sometimes an act of inhumanity would cause him to boil over with indignation. But, like all true moralists, he was an out-and-out opportunist. Like them, too, he hated the shams *of other people.* Candidly, I liked him when he wasn't preaching; and I realized all through that he was no more of a humbug than the folk who followed him to prison with their childish vituperations.

In addition to which, unlike them, he had a most winning disposition and a sterling character—when he was not engrossed in collecting sterling of another character! In short, he was very much like the finest specimens amongst his contemporaries—who could thank their stars they were fortunate enough not to have had his grievous temptations. . . .

§3

From Horatio Bottomley to Father Bernard

Vaughan may be thought a pretty big jump, but somehow they always seemed to me very much alike. They were both born tub-thumpers, both subject to transports of virtuous indignation, both fond of a drink, delightful companions, but inclined to be a bit quarrelsome in their cups ; both full of pity and practical assistance for anyone who was " down and out," both alternately pious and pagan, both intensely emotional and temperamental. They were far and away the best actors of their time (always excepting Lloyd George) and could have given points to any of their fellow-Thespians on the mimic stage.

I knew Father Bernard Vaughan very well indeed, but I am not going to attempt more than a sketch of him here. If I told all that I knew about him I would not be believed and would suffer the fate of all who try to tell the truth—that is, I would be accused of disparaging " a great and good man." Nothing could be further from my desire, for I was very fond of him ; but as the whole truth is impossible, I will oblige with a part of it, so that those who like their gods *neat* may not be alarmed.

Bernard Vaughan was a veritable social butterfly, a fact that no doubt helped him considerably when he began to denounce the sins of society. He knew his congregations through and through. Once I asked him whether he was not afraid of emptying his Mayfair church because of the offence he must be giving to ninety per cent of its frequenters.

" Offence ! " he cried. " They love it. It's a new sensation—being cursed for sins instead of being canvassed for alms. It's as much a luxury to them as fresh caviare. Why, I couldn't make more certain of filling the church to overflowing than by denouncing everyone who comes to listen to me."

He was right. . . .

" Do you sincerely believe," I asked him on another occasion, " that these society people you inveigh against with such violence are as bad as you make 'em out to be ? "

"Much worse ! " he promptly retorted. "But if I told them what I honestly thought of them and exposed their *real* vices, I'd be sequestered."

" But I should have thought the Church "—I commenced.

" The Church," he interrupted, " is of this world in so far as it has to deal with ordinary human beings. If it went too deep it might undermine itself. The Voice in the Wilderness is romantic but it cuts no ice."

" I thought "—I began again,

" That's your error," he came in quickly ; " you shouldn't think. Thought saps action. Not one man in a hundred thousand can think and do. The Church recognizes the limitations of men and helps them to surmount their mental obstacles by Faith. Why don't you join us ? The moment you become a child of the Church all your difficulties vanish into the air. The load of your solitary thoughts, too many and too heavy for you to bear, slips off you in an instant and a celestial comfort steals over you. The besetting horror of mental limitation becomes the beatific calm of spiritual consolation. It is like sitting back in your armchair, with your feet on the mantelpiece, a pipe in your mouth and a tankard of ale at your side—all your troubles, fears and dangers behind you—serene, happy and at peace for the remainder of your life."

I dutifully expressed my appreciation of the idyllic picture he had drawn, but confessed that my scepticism was temperamental and just as much a part of myself as the colour of my eyes or the length of my legs.

" Sheer heresy ! Sheer heresy ! ! " he exclaimed with uplifted hands. " It is your mental aberration that speaks. Your mind, unlike your body, is malleable——"

" You admit that ? " I broke in, scenting a slip and eager to trip him up, " then you must also admit " —but he was too quick for me.

" Of course I admit it," came the ready response ; " your mind is made malleable by God for His own purposes. But He only is the Hammer. And the question for you is : Will you let yourself be shaped by Him ? "

This struck me as a favourable moment for a drink, so we toddled off to a hotel in the vicinity and paid our respects to Bacchus.

§4

Now I must turn my attention to a few politicians. And I will begin with a man I knew better than any of those who follow him : Woodrow Wilson.

I first came into touch with him at Washington, when he was good enough to say he liked my company, and later in Paris at the Peace Conference. I am amused to read in my diary my original impression of him : " An unendurable pedagogue," was what I wrote. Which proves how hopelessly wrong original impressions may be. A week later I find this : " Had a ten-minutes chat with President Wilson. Can't quite make him out. Perhaps his intellectual snobbery is a mask for an ineradicable sensitiveness. He seems a decent sort, but his manner of laying down the law is intensely irritating. He appears to hover on the verge of saying something human, but never says it. And I can't get away from the feeling that he talks in order to hear himself speak."

Then, a month later, I am writing like this : " Half-an-hour with Wilson to-day. He grows upon me. At the end of our talk, I am positive he was close to intimacy. He seemed to be feeling his way. He *almost* said that, with a single exception, he couldn't trust a solitary senator ; but this was the extraordinarily roundabout way in which he put it—' It is difficult to be ever certain of touching the absolute truth among us here. The excuse may be that personal loyalty is at variance with public regard.

I do not know. Yet I can speak with conviction of one never-failing friend.' He's like that all the time. Is constitutionally incapable of speaking out. But I'm sure he wants to."

A fourth entry reveals a different man. There was a lapse of seven weeks between the last and what follows :

"Lunched at the White House. Wilson talked thirteen to the dozen all through the meal. Actually blackguarded the Germans in forthright style. Spoke for several minutes towards the close of the meal as though he were addressing a public meeting. His tone rather suggested that his guests were in opposition to his idealistic conception of a ' War to end war.' His peroration was delivered with amazing animation during dessert. While the rest of us were prosaically cracking nuts or peeling bananas, he soared into the ether of cosmic consciousness. ' And then,' said he with the true orator's emotional flourish, ' then we shall perhaps see the dawn of a better world. In it there will be little room for the fire-eater and peace-breaker. Others, I doubt not, if not we, the issue of our pain shall see. Then shall they know that dreams were dearer to us than dollars. Then, God willing, shall the strength of our arm be justified.'

"It was all we could do not to break out into applause. Perhaps it would have been better if we had done so, for the end of his speech (it was nothing less than a speech) was followed by a long and extremely awkward pause. The first man who spoke had such difficulty in ordering his voice for the occasion that it broke into a squeak and we all began to cough and chatter in order to cover it up. Shortly afterwards, the party broke up and Wilson begged me to come into his study for a few minutes. It may have been that his luncheon address had worked him up into an emotional condition. I can't say. Whatever the cause, he now, and for the first time in our intercourse, unbosomed himself to me."

Many of his comments on men and affairs were acute and prophetic, but most of them were far too intimate to be broadcast until their subjects have followed him to the grave. Nevertheless I can illustrate his shrewdness when at a distance from certain contemporaries ; it was in keen contrast with his obtuseness when at close quarters with them. This will furnish another proof that Shakespeare knew what he was talking about when he made Macbeth say of Banquo :

> . . . . under him
> My Genius is rebuked, as it is said
> Mark Antony's was by Cæsar.

It is a curious fact, attested throughout history, that men who are perfectly well able to appreciate one another when apart are totally unable to do one another justice when together. Each in his own way may have talents above the ordinary, but

somehow the virtues of each are cancelled out by
contact with those of the other. This is also the
chief reason why a great collaboration in art or
action is the rarest thing in the world.

Here are President Wilson's estimates of two
public men before he had met them, given to me in
the privacy of his sanctum :

" I doubt if I would like Mr. Lloyd George. He
has a way of appealing to the emotions and not to
the intellect which I distrust. At a time like this it
is vital that we should keep our heads. He is, I
should guess, too charming to be safe."

" I have given care to the study of Clemenceau.
He is a man who cannot see further than the frontiers
of France. He can see them very distinctly to the
north, to the south, and to the west ; but his sight
is misty when he looks towards the east, due no
doubt to the haze that hangs over the Rhine. He is
what is known as a realist—that is, a man who knows
that two and two make four. Alas ! there are
others who can count as well, and it is because they
all count alike that we have wars."

Later, when I met Wilson in Paris, he had considerably altered his opinions, but the revised versions
of the above were far from improvements. Lloyd
George had already captured him—he admitted as
much—and he honestly believed that he had only
to take the British Prime Minister's advice in order
to establish the Kingdom of God on earth. Clemenceau on the other hand frightened him—he admitted

that, too—and he told me that the Frenchman was " immovable as a mountain."

I can still see Wilson as he sat one day in the room of a hotel, towards the end of the Conference. He sat disconsolately, chin on breast, talking at times almost monosyllabically, with his legs thrust out before him. He had just been advised by his secretary to eat his lunch, but he shook his head and said :

" It can wait."

I asked him if he were tired.

" Not tired," he answered, " but weary."

As he said it there was a wealth of meaning in the phrase.

A little later, as we were going down to lunch, he took my arm and said almost inaudibly :

" I have tried . . . . tried . . . . but I do not know that I have done my best."

A strange confession from a man who had breathed nothing but idealism for two years.

Like most super-sensitive people, Wilson was quickly converted by storm and stress into a weak-kneed bully. He mustn't be judged too harshly for being utterly unfit to grapple with the political brigands on whose side, to his utter consternation, he found himself.

It was, I am afraid, the old, old story. A dreamer had come into touch with reality, had awakened, and had forgotten his dream. . . .

§5

It is almost incredible that two such dissimilar types could be found in the same world as Woodrow Wilson and Georges Clemenceau. They differed so radically in temperament, outlook, manners, habits, in all the qualities of brain and heart. Indeed, they might almost be said to belong to different species.

Clemenceau was never happy when he was not fighting, and for the greater part of his life he had his teeth, bull-dog fashion, well into the calves of one or other of his compatriots. He was a first-class duellist, with sword and pistol, and when he couldn't use those weapons he used to fall back upon his pen or his tongue—which if anything were deadlier still !

He was never popular in France because his wit spared no one and was of a peculiarly bitter kind. Once stung, never forgotten. His writings reveal an almost brutally disillusioned nature, and this was true of the man, who was a stark and cynical realist. I once heard him tell a story which he afterwards, I believe, dramatized for the stage. I give a synopsis of it :

A blind Chinaman, wonderfully happy in the love of his wife, his friends and his poetry, suddenly recovers his sight. Instantly he finds out that his wife is the mistress of his best friend and that his paid companion is cheating him of his fame as a poet. Other horrible facts are laid bare to him and at length he blinds himself again voluntarily, saying as he does so: "To be happy, one must be blind."

That story is characteristic of Clemenceau's outlook upon life. But an incident in the Chamber paints him still more vividly and accounts for his persistent unpopularity. When he came to power during the war, some socialist asked him what he intended to do. He answered: "I have only one object at present—to win the war and clear France of its invaders." Then, speaking to the whole House, he added: "When I have done this, you may proceed to pass a vote of censure on me, and I haven't the least doubt that it will be carried unanimously by all my dear friends who now cheer me to the echo."

Imagine our Lloyd Georges and Winston Churchills talking like that in the Commons! To be quite candid, however, it didn't go down particularly well even in France where they admire causticity.

Practically every day while he was in office in 1918 he visited the front to confer with Foch or some other commander, in addition to his ordinary work. Pretty good going for a septuagenarian, but his vitality was always his strongest point. I remember him telling me that he had once fulfilled an assignation, fought a duel, attended a cabinet meeting, addressed a public gathering, inspected a new building, entertained a Foreign Ambassador, sat through a theatrical performance, and carried out the routine work of his department—all in one day. Unless I am mistaken, and I don't think I am, he was over sixty at the time!

His refreshing cynicism darted out in every direction during a lunch to which he had invited me. It was quite an informal affair and Georges was at the top of his form, playful and indiscreet.

Someone asked him why he had always been so disliked by the populace.

" Because I tell them the truth," he replied.

" But why are you disliked by the politicians ? " he was asked.

" Because I am incorruptible," he flashed back.

" Are you, then, the only honest politician in France ? "

" But no ! They are all honest "—a slight pause —" until temptation comes their way."

" So you are the only one who has survived office with a clean conscience ? "

" Perhaps. But then, you know, my wants are few."

" Otherwise—— ? "

" I should not have gone into politics."

" What, then ? "

" High finance."

We all laughed.

I had long wanted to know why he had made no attempt to shoot Paul Déroulède when they had a duel. In one of those scenes so dear to the French heart, Paul had accused him of being a traitor and he had retaliated with " You're a liar ! " Following this pleasant little exchange of confidences in the best Gallic manner, they met, and Clemenceau, who was a dead shot, discharged his pistol into the air. I therefore asked him for an explanation of his clemency.

"Why should I wish to shoot the only honest politician in France?" he countered.

"But what about him?"

"He was in exactly the same case," replied Clemenceau; "he had no wish to shoot the only other."

"Then did you arrange it between yourselves?"

"Naturally we couldn't risk the future of France by leaving it to chance. But Paul was the soul of honour and privately told me that he'd shoot me with the greatest pleasure in the world if I felt at all sore over his treatment of me."

Someone—an Englishman—said that duels nowadays were very childish affairs, and that no one took them seriously.

"Speaking from your own inexperience, I suppose?" lunged Clemenceau.

The other had no answer, but forced a laugh and bided his time. It came at last. We had all been talking about religion, and suddenly Clemenceau said:

"We have no puritans in France, except our English and American visitors, and they don't behave like puritans when they come here."

"No, indeed," chimed in the fellow who had

been previously sat upon, " they have little incentive
to behave decently in Paris."

"Dear, dear!" remarked Clemenceau sweetly.
"I had no idea their own women-folk were so
unattractive. You surprise me."

Upon which clearly-struck and highly characteristic
note I think I had better leave Georges Clemenceau.

§6

One of the most curious phenomena in the history
of British politics is the almost unaccountable failure
of the Labour leaders to retain their influence over
their followers. This can only be understood when
the personalities of the chief leaders are understood.
After all, they had every opportunity to keep the
confidence of the Party. Had they shown any real
initiative when they were in power, had they given
a glimpse of a constructive policy to solve the
pressing social problems of the hour, had they done
a single thing that any Liberal Government would
not have done equally well, they might have swept
the country and returned to office with a handsome
majority. Instead of which, so wretchedly did they
fail to do anything worth doing, that the mere
publication of a letter by their opponents swept
them from power. In other words the voters merely
wanted an excuse to get rid of them, and the
Conservative Party very kindly obliged them with
that excuse.

It is worth our while trying to understand these men whose signal failure to succeed where success seemed inevitable gives them an honoured niche in the fane of political futilities. Think of their chances! A young and energetic Party behind them—a sympathetic if watchful country at their back—the sponsorship of one of the two big historic Parties to depend upon—and what was the result? Nothing! But stay—let us be just. They increased our freedom in one very memorable way. They permitted taxi-cabs to go through Hyde Park; and, lest there were any danger of our forgetting for an instant the din of Oxford Street, we were henceforth free to enjoy it also in the one place to which some selfish and unsocial people used to retire for peace and quiet.

Ramsay MacDonald is as niggardly of confidences as his fellow-countrymen are supposed to be of cash. He is by nature far too secretive to make a good Prime Minister. Not once did he open his heart to his colleagues during the Labour Administration. He was perhaps the first Prime Minister in the history of this country who talked less at cabinet meetings than any of his fellow-ministers. If he hadn't been such an extremely pleasant fellow personally, there would have been serious trouble. As it was, there were sporadic outbreaks of ill-humour and adverse commentary.

Naturally he got the reputation even on the Front Bench of being autocratic—Snowden practically called him an autocrat to his face on one occasion, and there was a slight flare-up—which spread leftwards throughout the entire Party until, if it hadn't been for the difficulty of replacing him without splitting the Party in two, he would most certainly have been shelved.

I met Ramsay twice during his term of office, and I must confess to liking him very much. He seemed to me to possess style without affectation. I mean he really does impress one without the aid of artifice. Simple, direct, sincere and thoroughly honest, he has in addition a native courtesy that seldom goes with the higher virtues. But I could see wherein his weakness as a leader lay. Too frequently he used the first person singular instead of the first person plural when speaking for the Government. A mere technical blemish of course, but significant in that it denoted that very " the Government—it is I " attitude to which his followers so strongly objected.

The truth is—I could see it quite plainly at the time—he has a trait in his nature common to most big leaders (worse than useless in a democratic State) : he cannot trust anyone to do a job except himself. That was his weakness as Prime Minister. He lost the confidence of the Party because he would not take the Party into his confidence.

That is where a Lloyd George has the advantage over a MacDonald. The former picked his men well, gave them *carte blanche* and damned the consequences. The latter chose his men weakly, restricted their range of activities wherever possible—and dreaded the consequences. Yet MacDonald is a very much finer specimen of humanity than Lloyd George. Perhaps his very conscientiousness let him down. The good qualities in a man may be bad qualities in a ruler—and vice versa. . . . .

§7

Philip Snowden is the exact opposite to his leader. He is only too anxious to take people's advice at every step, to confide in them and to receive their confidences. He is all for making every difficulty a round-table conference matter. And that is *his* weakness. He has little self-reliance. He hovers perpetually between extremes, unconvinced that one is right, and equally unconvinced that the other is wrong. What convictions he has were obtained from books; but he might at any moment cease to hold those convictions if he were to read other books.

To give a concrete example: before becoming the Chancellor of the Exchequer he was an out-and-out believer in the power of the State and the right of the State to issue credit and manipulate its own finances. Several round-table conferences with leading bankers and financiers resulted in his becoming an out-and-out believer in the power and sole right of those gentry to issue credit and manipulate the finances.

Yet so used are we to accept the public statements of ministers and financiers on matters of credit as unexceptionable, that not a single newspaper in Great Britain commented adversely on Snowden's statement that the bankers would find in the Labour Party their best friends.

As an ordinary social being Snowden is not particularly attractive. I have met him quite formally at 10, Downing Street and I had a longish chat with him at a Buckingham Palace garden-party. On the latter occasion he was distinctly impressed by his surroundings, and the black wrath of earlier years had wholly given way to the roseate hues of a dignified maturity. I recall a gesture of his which took in the Palace, its garden, the King and Queen, the gaily-dressed throng, and everything else in the immediate vicinity, even the uniforms of the bandsmen; and as his arm began its all-embracing sweep, he began to speak :

" A wonderful pageant, is it not ? There is something in history, in tradition, after all. There will always be a reigning house in this country, because it is a picturesque and quite harmless symbol—the sole remaining one—of our past. It links us visibly with our ancestors. It is the outward manifestation of our race-consciousness."

I couldn't help wondering what Philip the Younger, socialist, would have said to Philip the Elder, royalist. . . .

§8

In a phrase or two I can explain the failure of the other Labour leaders to capture the loyalty of their Party. Thomas failed because he was too popular with his opponents. Clynes failed because his mediocrity was a little too obvious. Wheatley failed because, being a Roman Catholic, and therefore antagonistic to Birth Control, he was out of touch with the progressive spirit of his side. Henderson failed because he was popular like Thomas, mediocre like Clynes, and reactionary like Wheatley. The rest don't count—except that man whose spirit pervaded the entire Party and whose personality would be enough to wreck a stronger team than Labour put into the field when he was President of the Board of Trade.

Sidney Webb is the St. Paul of Socialism. Like St. Paul he has severely qualified the teaching of the Master, and has issued to the Faithful what might be termed a series of " Epistles to the Fabians," in which the Gospel according to St. Marx has been watered down to the less astringent needs of the bourgeois class.

Webb is a dry-as-dust, humdrum, static individual. No, I am wrong! That is the whole point. Whatever else he may or may not be, the one thing he most indubitably is *not* is an " individual." He is absolutely devoid of individuality. There is a sort of plurality about him. True, he has features that approximate to the human variety ; but in actual fact he is a " collective " phenomenon, a generalized specialist.

When I said to him one day, " I doubt very much if humanity really wants Socialism," he replied, " Humanity doesn't know what it wants and therefore

should be given what is good for it." There you
have Webb in a sentence. And it is this soullessness
of his that has damped the enthusiasm of the Party,
clamped its energies within the rigid bands of an
unadaptable creed, and vamped a threadbare doctrine
with economic facings of very questionable currency.

There will be no life in Socialism until its adherents
become socialized—that is individualized—that is
humanized—and there will be no hope for it while
its major prophet is Sidney Webb, who is the reverse
of all this. He irritates the majority of human beings
who meet him, and only gets on well with machines.
He is a bore in private and a bore on the platform.
He is the type of man whom we all know as "an
official," the type that makes all of us dread our
dealings with governments : because the only alternative to ceasing our dealings and swallowing our
wrongs is to murder the official !

This fearfully fallible being, with his static creed,
his rigid dogma, his still-born economic faith, constitutes within himself the finest advertisement for
his opponents. They have only to point at him
and say, "That's what they want us to be like—a
standardized Webb," for everyone who has ever
entered a post office to walk straight to the polling-
station and register a defiant negative.

But I must be just and remember that he has
immolated himself all his life on the altar of Webbism,
which, after all, called for an almost unbearable
degree of pluck, perseverance and pessimism. . . .

CHAPTER XII

THE SOAP KING

Lord Leverhulme

STRANGELY enough—or not strangely—my diary is singularly free from entries dealing with the outstanding figures in the industrial world. This is not really surprising because so few of them, when met, are found to be outstanding. The late Lord Leverhulme, however, was an exception. Like all successful business magnates, he was at heart a collector. He collected pictures, statuary, china, books, businesses and men. In a word he was acquisitive.

But there was nothing miserly about him. Not for him the secret gloating over some priceless *objet d'art*. He liked his left hand to know what his right hand was doing. With his right hand he acquired— with his left he exhibited or gave. His was an ingenuous nature. He certainly did not believe in hiding his light under a bushel; it flamed there for all to see, and shone with equal vividness on factories, warehouses, plantations, model villages, schools and art galleries. There was not a sphere of human endeavour in which he did not attempt to make his mark—and leave his mark.

Lord Leverhulme was not a man of one fixed idea, but a man of many fixed ideas ; and once he had set his heart upon a thing, heaven help anyone who tried to prevent him from acquiring it or achieving it ! That's why Parliament was such a disappointment to him. Ready to hack his way through mountains of opposition in the commercial world, he found himself lost and helpless in the jungle of politics. Able to bluff to any extent over a business deal, he was not equipped for the super-bluff of parliamentary procedure. More than a match for a recalcitrant shareholder or a revolting colleague, he was quite at sea when it came to dealing with the artificial antagonisms of the House.

In other words, he was a realist. In business he no sooner saw the end than he imagined the means. In politics he found that the means were usually the only end, and that the last thing wanted was a solution of any of the problems that confronted the different parties. This staggered him, and it is a lasting mystery to many of his admirers that he remained so staunch a friend of that strange political personage who symbolized everything that he most loathed in politics—Lloyd George. The explanation perhaps is that he was so amazed and delighted to find that a politician could get anything done at all, that Lloyd George's war record wiped out for him all his previous miserable experiences.

Perhaps another reason for Lord Leverhulme's political failure was due to the fact that he could never really imagine himself in any other position than that of Prime Minister. The Autocrat of the Board Meeting became confused and wretched when he found himself just one of six hundred whose business was certainly not to reason why. It was a cause of secret relief among his friends and admirers when he left the political stage. His ultimate re-appearance as a decorative figure in the House of Lords must have given him a deal of quiet satisfaction. He had an impish sense of humour. By the way, at about the time of his elevation to the peerage, the wife of a Scottish nobleman, upon being informed that Sir William Lever was taking the title of " Lord Leverhulme of the Western Isles," remarked somewhat tartly that she thought " Lord Lather'em of the Wash " would be more appropriate. In spite of the fact that I had some sympathy with the Scottish point of view in regard to his lordship's title, I hope this rather unkind remark never reached his ears—amusing though it certainly was. Somehow I don't think that even his sense of humour would have risen to it.

Of his various business successes I am not qualified to speak, and, as it happens, they do not interest me. It is in the man whom I met on perhaps a dozen different occasions that my interest is centred. I was once present at some charity function in the gardens of " The Hill," Hampstead. Various semi-royal personages were there, and one of them was good enough to tell his lordship that I was interested in pictures.

" Come along, then," he said ; " these people can easily manage without me. As a matter of fact, they don't really want me at all—it's my garden they want."

One story of that walk through his private collection will suffice to show his attitude towards art. Firstly came a genuine joy in possession ; secondly, to my astonishment, he displayed what I shall call a literary or anecdotal interest. With every picture came a little story about how he obtained it, in what circumstances it was painted, and so on. Rarely if ever was the picture allowed to speak for itself. Lastly— and I was glad to note that it was so—came the question of price. Unlike another millionaire whom I know, Lord Leverhulme did not dismiss a whole wall of pictures with the comment : " There's £25,000 on that wall ! "

I remember we paused longest in front of " The Black Brunswicker," while Lord Leverhulme told me how Dickens's niece (I think it was) had posed for the lady, and had never seen the man who had posed for the soldier. This appeared to him to be of greater interest than the picture itself ; though he pointed out to me the painting of a fold in the silken dress as a masterpiece of . . . . the painting of folds in silken dresses.

We moved on slowly, and rounding a corner came

upon a man standing with his back to us and looking out of a window. He turned at the sound of our footsteps. Immediately one light went out of Lord Leverhulme's eyes. It was the light in the eyes of a host being pleasant to a guest. And it was replaced by what looked suspiciously like the light of battle.

" You'll excuse me now," said Leverhulme to me, in what I took to be his business tone of voice. He then shook hands with me and turned towards the man. As I retraced my steps I heard that same business voice saying :

" It's no better to be early than late. I said *half-past-four* ! "

Lord Leverhulme was evidently far away from the world of art. . . .

For art in its cultural sense I cannot imagine that he had much personal use. But that he realized its value in this connection must be undisputed. Granted that he wanted his epitaph to be the same as Wren's —*Si monumentum requiris, circumspice*—yet his inclusion of an art gallery in his village of Port Sunlight argued something finer in his character than a desire for mere personal glory.

Many people, I know, have insisted that he put himself out of court forever as a serious respecter of the art of painting by his mutilation of Augustus John's portrait of him. But this is a stupid and superficial criticism. Lord Leverhulme did not mutilate the John portrait because he didn't respect it, but because he did. No man, I should think, knew his own weaknesses better than he. Through all his generosity there ran a streak of ruthlessness. The good qualities that made for success were balanced by others that warded off failure. It was these last that John brought out in his painting, and looking upon it Lord Leverhulme saw himself as he did not like to be—as, indeed, he tried hard not to be. And this, I imagine, is what he said to himself :

" This shall not be posterity's conception of me, because it will not be true. This is the part that I have buried in order that posterity may enjoy what the finer part will give it. For this to come to light in later years will be a libel on me dead, though it may be true of me living. I will have my portrait painted by De Laszlo."

Although I met Lord Leverhulme on several occasions after this episode, I never once broached the subject. I thought of the business voice telling me to mind my own business. All the above, therefore, is pure theory, but not, I believe, the less true on that account.

For Leverhulme everything had to have a purpose. Just as " art for art's sake " was to him a meaningless and silly phrase—and, as he said, " an excuse for painting things that won't sell "—so literature was principally " information." He had no use for atmosphere. If he read a novel, which was seldom, it was to learn something about his fellow-man or woman. Mostly he read history or biography and would at times talk interestingly about both. But he once said to an unsuccessful novelist to whom he had given a job: " I don't think you'll regret going into business. Literature's a very nice ornamental walking-stick, but it's a poor crutch."

Science to him was chiefly the servant of industry. Its function was to evolve new products and new methods of obtaining them. Perhaps his nearest approach to the humanities was through architecture. He was, I believe, a F.R.I.B.A. At any rate, he once told me that he was an architect and that the designing of Port Sunlight was very much the work of his own hand. But then architecture, of all the arts, has the most obvious purpose. A house is to live in. A factory is to work in. A church is to worship in. They may incidentally be beautiful, but their prime reason for existence is Use.

As an illustration of Lord Leverhulme's attitude to art and life, here is a story told me by a young friend—an artist—who obtained an introduction to him in the hope of getting a commission. To his surprise, Leverhulme gave him a personal interview and started right off by saying:

" Can you sell your pictures ? "

The young man was completely taken off his balance, and stammered something about not having sold many but that he hoped he'd make his way in time, and so forth.

Leverhulme thereupon treated him to the following homily :

" I don't know why it is that artists think they can paint what people don't want and still take up an attitude of annoyance when nobody'll buy their stuff. Remember this, young man "—and he tapped the bunched fingers of his right hand into the open palm of his left—" an artist who's not a salesman is only half an artist. What'd be the good of my making soap if I couldn't sell it? Everybody has got to be a salesman. You come down off your high horse and try to sell something."

Thoroughly bewildered by this time, my young friend mumbled that he hoped to sell something to his lordship.

" P'raps you will some day," was the reply, "p'raps you will—but go away and learn how to do it first."

Then, without giving the by-now pulverized artist time to say anything more, he beamed at him, shook his hand, and said :

" Very glad to have seen you. Tell Mr. X I'm obliged to him for sending you along."

This was his usual formula to denote an interview was at an end.

My young friend was thoroughly puzzled and wretched, but I suspect that Leverhulme had done a bit of quick sizing-up, had accurately estimated what was unhappily the truth—that he was not talking to a genius—and had acted in what he thought the kindest manner. The whole episode, however, reveals his philosophy and general attitude towards life—which was a purely utilitarian one.

This may have been why he considered the Americans the greatest race in the world. I happened to meet him shortly after my return from the Washington Conference. He asked me how I liked the States, and I told him. Then he said :

" Everybody ought to go to America at least once a year to brighten up their ideas."

" Possibly," I said, " but I'm afraid I didn't go there for that reason."

" Well, then, go there again for it ! " he answered abruptly, and strode away.

One aspect of the man I must not omit. One of his hobbies was the collecting of funny stories— preferably of the *double entendre* type. The moment he heard a yarn of this description, out came his pocket-book and he would ask the teller to repeat it while he wrote it down. I actually witnessed this at a luncheon party. A fellow began to tell him an amusing story. He instantly became interested, brought out his pocket-book, and begged the other to let him have it verbatim. The incident aroused the attention of the entire table, because the yarn-spinner had to bellow the words of his yarn, very deliberately, into his lordship's deaf ear. I need not say that, on the occasion of the repetition, it lost a little of its humorous quality !

I have said that Lord Leverhulme was a collector, and I could never escape from the feeling that he invited hoards of people to his house, not for any pleasure it might have given them, but for the

pleasure it gave him in his capacity of collector.
I fear, too, that upon occasion the parties he gave
at " The Hill " could only be described as " a
collection."

The Queen, by the way, was very fond of him, and
he displayed with pride a beautiful bowl that she
had given him.   Indeed, the fact that he was smiled
upon by royalty was proved by the acceptance of a
seat on the Board of Lever Bros. by the Marquis of
Carisbrooke.   Nevertheless I cannot help thinking
that the Marquis had to put considerable restraint
upon his feelings when he was invited to " The
Hill " one day and found that he and his lady were
expected to make themselves pleasant to the back-
row of a beauty chorus !   There were certainly times
when the Soap King's vulgarianism was a little too
exuberant. . . .

The last time I met Lord Leverhulme was about a
year before his death at a public dinner.   As a matter
of fact, I was sitting next to him.   But as I happened
to be on his deaf side, the conversation was limited
to my bright smiling nods as I acquiesced in some of
his caustic criticisms of politicians and diplomats.
He never failed to let me know, in a delightful and
humorous way, that he held me and my kind in
the utmost contempt—from a utilitarian point of
view—though socially he admitted that he found most
of us pleasant.   But the difference between his
contempt and that of Cecil Rhodes was that while
Rhodes despised us, was rude to us, and used us,

Leverhulme despised us, was charming to us, and
never used us!

His opinion of government officials generally was
never more forcibly expressed than in his bout with
the Governor of Nigeria, whose administration he
accused of making business impossible in that vast
region. His innocent surprise when the Governor
refused a personal invitation to dinner on his yacht
was characteristic. He could not understand why
abuse of the official should be taken as an insult
to the man. To him, with his balanced and practical
mind, they were two different beings.

The dinner was a rather tedious affair, and the
moment the speeches began Lord Leverhulme grew
restless. Every now and then he would scribble a
little note on a piece of paper and put it back into
his pocket. Then he would sit for a moment absolutely still, but making the gentleman who was
exactly opposite him acutely uncomfortable by staring
some hundreds of miles *through* him. He hadn't the
slightest idea of the strain and disturbance he was
causing in the breast on the other side of the cloth.
I imagine that he was in the Congo or even the
South Seas. Wherever it was, it was a long way
off. . . .

A vibration of the table as one speaker sat down
and another got up would bring him back through
the ether and he would sit tapping the long-nailed
fingers of his right hand on the table. Not for him
the anodyne of alcohol or nicotine; and, to be

perfectly truthful, I don't think he needed it. He hadn't got to speak on this occasion, and he was merely waiting until a general movement of chairs released him from the necessity of thinking in uncongenial surroundings.

The quiet drumming of his finger-nails on the table became faintly audible once or twice, and it gave me a wicked pleasure to note that it put Sir ——, who was not in his best post-prandial form, rather off his stroke. Between his " er . . . . ers . . .." the speaker glanced at the offending hand, but to no purpose—and eventually he struggled through to a finish.

The last speech began; Lord Leverhulme made another note. A look of pleasure came into his eyes. He had evidently solved a problem. With a brighter face he surveyed the table. A flattering reference had just been made to himself. But he had not heard it. He was pleased about something else—quite unconnected with the dinner, I am sure.

The speaker made a neat little peroration. Lord Leverhulme was once more tapping the table. His lips were pursed. What new train of thought was this, I wondered? The speaker came to an end and sat down. There was a rumble of " hear hears," which gradually died away. There was silence.

At least for a fraction of a second there *seemed* to be silence.

But suddenly I, and everyone else at that table, became conscious of another kind of entertainment.

I turned and looked at Lord Leverhulme. His lordship's lips were still pursed. Happily oblivious of everything around him, the great industrial magnate was whistling softly to himself. The tune, I believe, was " Poor old Joe ! "

Such happiness, I thought, boded ill for some competitor on the morrow. . . .

CHAPTER XIII

GLIMPSES

Lady Astor, Margot Asquith, The Countess of Warwick, Max Beerbohm, Walter H. Page, James McNeill Whistler, Augustus John.

IT is only natural that in the course of my duties I should have made a number of casual acquaintanceships which have never ripened into any degree of intimacy. Of such were most of those brief contacts with literary men which I have described in my chapter entitled "Scribblers." There are many isolated entries in my diary beginning in this sort of way: "Met —— at Lady ——'s luncheon party to-day." And ending, perhaps, with a short conversation which I was able to snatch with the subject of the entry.

As I have always been a most determined diarist, many of these " glimpses " (as I shall call them here) are simply silly. Looking back over them now, I cannot help wondering what could have persuaded me to record them. Just to give an instance :

" Met Whistler strolling along the embankment.

We smiled at one another, and I said ' How do you do ?' He replied 'I don't'—and passed on."

Now why did I take the trouble to commit that absurdity to paper ? I cannot honestly answer. But it is typical of many.

There are, on the other hand, quite a few " glimpses" of interest and possibly even of value. These have gone to the writing of this last chapter. I have expanded them all with my fuller knowledge of the subjects concerned, though none of them has ever done more than flit across the stage of my personal experience.

§1

No one, least of all a positive personality, ever strikes any two people in exactly the same way. There are a hundred facets to most people's characters and one can seldom prognosticate how so-and-so will behave under any given conditions. For example, the portrait of Lord Northcliffe which I have attempted in this book struck one reader, a friend of his lordship's, as a gross caricature. But the reason for that was obvious. He never saw Lord Northcliffe in the kind of situation that I have described. He probably only knew him as a host, and he forgot in the heat of the moment that I had called " The Napoleon of Fleet Street " an admirable host.

Thus it might even be true to say that a ma'sn closest friends know least about him. I am not trying to be paradoxical. I am merely trying to point out a common misconception and explain why it is common. You think you know all about a man because you see a lot of him at the club, where he is probably at his best. But how does he strike the people who work under him? And how does he strike the people who work over him? And how does he strike the people who work *with* him? I am pretty certain that he strikes them all in totally different ways. Why, we even show different aspects of ourselves to different friends. So how on earth can we expect anyone to get at the full truth about ourselves?

A great biographer must reconcile all these aspects of a man. We who content ourselves with sketching a few of them do not profess to say the last word about anyone. We can only help the biographer to paint his composite portrait. And so you must not be surprised if you read that some of the characteristics I have exposed here are not recognized by friends who thought they knew the folk concerned. Indeed, I should be greatly surprised if my efforts received the approbation of half those readers whose personal knowledge justifies their criticism.

The above remarks must be kept carefully in mind by readers of this chapter, because the ensuing " glimpses " may frequently appear to contradict the general impression that has been formed relative to the characters and attainments of those whom I now introduce. Especially will this be the case with

Lady Astor, who has the reputation of being an altruist in every sense of the word, whereas I am convinced that what passes for altruism is simply an extreme form of egotism.

Lady Astor brought with her from America the zeal of the reformer who knows what is good for everybody else ! She is a strange mixture of humility and pride. Humble in that she feels she is guided by providence. Proud in that she is convinced she is its chosen instrument. She makes one feel that no doubt ever enters her mind that she was sent into the world, not only with the object of making it a better place, but with a very definite knowledge of the simple steps whereby its betterment can be effected.

She has two mottoes : (1) *Sic vos non vobis*, which of course applies to the lower orders ; and (2) *Nemo me impune lacessit*, which applies to herself. Yet I wouldn't like to say she's not sincere. In fact I think she would be prepared to sacrifice for her opinions every mortal thing—except her power to inflict them on others.

Her prevailing weakness, assuming that what I have already said may be accounted for strength, is a child-like and rather taking vanity. I call it child-like because it reminds me of nothing so much as the delight a child takes in exhibiting its strength. She likes to suggest hidden sources of power and influence. She really does love to think that she can do whatever she sets out to do.

Now and again, in the course of conversation, when someone has asked a question to which no one can give an answer, she will say " Ah ! " in such a way as to hint that she alone could provide the answer if she wanted to.

I recall an occasion when she dropped a hint in this fashion three times at a single sitting. It was shortly after the action against Horatio Bottomley had been begun. Someone at table remarked that the issue lay in the balance, because Bottomley had got out of worse holes than this one.

" He won't get out of this one," came tartly from Lady Astor.

" Indeed ? " queried the other, " and why not ? "

" *Vous-verrez*," answered her ladyship, shaking her head and smiling inscrutably.

A little later the misdeeds of a certain politician were being discussed, and Lady Astor interrupted an argument of pros and cons with :

" It doesn't much matter. He will resign shortly, and before a year is out people will have forgotten his name."

" How do you know that ? " was the eager question from all sides.

" I just know it," she returned ; and the air of mystery with which she managed in those four words to surround the subject was truly remarkable.

Later still the inevitable topic of Prohibition was started. Many tongues wagged, but Lady Astor sat in silence until the matter had been thoroughly thrashed out and the opposing sides had agreed to disagree. Then her voice was heard :

" It's merely a matter of time. It's coming for sure. We "—(there was a slight emphasis on the " we " and a repetition of it)—" we will force the issue sooner or later."

" But surely," said a stalwart Tory peer who was sitting on her right, " you cannot force a measure on an unwilling people in these democratic days ? "

" The unwilling people, as you call them, are not sufficiently unwilling to go to the poll and signify as much. All reforms are brought about by the energy of the reformers, and indirectly by the apathy of their opponents, who are always in a majority. You remember the parable of the judge who yielded, not to the justice of a complaint, but to the importunacy of the complainant. People will sacrifice anything, even liberty, for peace and a quiet life. Reformers rightly bank on the boredom of the anti-reformers. Progress is only possible through the ennui of the reactionaries. ' Ask and ye shall receive ' is true enough—only you've got to go on asking. We have the money and we have the will, and time is therefore on our side."

" But," pursued the peer, " suppose the others put up some money and suppose they develop a will ? You aren't reckoning on that."

" We will win in the long run, whatever happens."

" You think you will."

" I *know* we will."

" The brewers, then, are for sale ? "

" Ah ! "

She wouldn't continue the topic, and of course the implication of that " Ah ! " was clearly an affirmative. The result was that nearly all of us came away with the firm impression that Lady Astor had a finger on every pulse of the national life. Which, I am convinced, was precisely the impression she wished to convey. An excusable vanity, perhaps, but there was at any rate one person upon whom it did not altogether impose.

§2

Most people have got a pretty clear idea of Margot Asquith in their heads by now. If they haven't, it certainly isn't her fault. Within certain well-defined limits she has painted herself fairly well in her auto-biography. The truth is there right enough—though most of it is carefully hidden between the lines.

One of her earliest admirers and oldest friends, Lord Balfour, read the book with keen interest and remarked when he had finished it; " So that is Margot ! A vivid personality certainly. I must obtain an introduction to her."

Yet it would be wrong to say that she doesn't behave in real life in much the same way as she reports herself behaving in the book. The chief difference is that in the book she is seldom silly, whereas in real life she is seldom subtle.

One of her favourite poses is that she is unpopular. But therein she flatters herself. I have never heard anyone say anything against her except that she talks far too much, and says far too little ; but that is the only serious complaint I have ever heard against her.

Next to celebrity-hunting, which has been her life-long hobby, her quaintest quality has been a pretended preoccupation with the things of the mind and the spirit. Perhaps it is impossible to collect celebrities—especially those in the world of art— if you do not profess a keen sympathy with the profundities, an intuitive comprehension of the sources of inspiration. Be that as it may, Margot has always made a point of discussing theology or poetry with the zest most women would bring to a new hat or the latest dance.

The truth is that she must be in the swim, even at the risk of being out of her depth. Other women content themselves with paddling in the shallows of fashion. Margot is not satisfied unless she can battle her way through the currents of science, the eddies of art, and the whirlpools of religion. She must therefore know personally—indeed intimately—all the leaders of thought and action, carry them off into remote corners, pump them thoroughly, and return (refreshed by long draughts of philosophy, or cant) to exchange scandal with Lady Di.

I was present at an amusing encounter between Margot and Canon Scott Holland. The latter, though

a fashionable preacher and something of a social
butterfly, never could put a safeguard upon his
tongue. Though usually honey-mouthed, he was
capable upon occasion of bursting out with unplea-
santries in a voice that could be heard through the
door of a safe.

" At last I have been able to tear myself away ! "
she exclaimed. " And now for our little talk. I
have been looking forward to it all the evening."

" Then let the subject be horses," muttered the
Canon.

" Horses ? " cried Margot.

" Horses," assented the Canon.

" But why horses ? " insisted the lady.

" Because you can do all the talking. I know
nothing whatever about the brutes."

" Oh ! " from Margot in keen disappointment.

" Tit-for-tat, dear lady," concluded Scott Holland ;
" last time I discoursed on the Reformation about
which you knew nothing ; now it's your turn to do
the talking and mine to do the nodding."

They then moved out of my hearing, but as I saw
Mrs. Asquith chatting with Sir Edward Grey a few
minutes later, I assumed that the Canon's suggestion
had failed to mature.

I still refer to her as Mrs. Asquith because I never
knew her as anything else. The " Margot Tennant "
days were before my time in the Diplomatic Service
and I have only once clapped eyes on her since her
elevation, when I heard her introduce herself to a

man in Switzerland as " The Countess of Oxford—
Mrs. Asquith, you know."

The first thing a stranger would notice about her
would be, I am sure, her vivacity. In vulgar parlance
she can talk the hind legs off a donkey, and her
stream of enthusiastic nothings can sometimes be
quite inspiriting. The second time I ever met her—
at a luncheon-party in Cavendish Square, where the
Asquiths then lived—I was almost carried away by
the flow of her eloquence. She was witty, too, and
I entered in my diary a couple of her sayings that
struck me at the time as distinctly above the level of
most prandial-patter. One was :

" Intellect without imagination is like soup
without salt. However fine the quality, there is no
savour."

The other was :

" Literature is the greatest art in the world, because
one can only define the other arts through the medium
of speech."

Someone countered the last statement with : " But
does not the highest art transcend speech ? "

Mrs. Asquith answered :

" Then it is not universal. The emotions it arouses
may be entirely different in different people. Surely
the greatest art is that to which the greatest number
of people respond in much about the same way.
The nature of their response can only be defined in
words."

This of course is strictly true. The things that

remain, the things that go deepest to the root of our common experience, are the greatest things—and the very meaning of the word " great " suggests something of universal application. Take the case of the late war. It is not the songs or the pictures it inspired that remain, but the phrases. " The Contemptible Little Army," which apparently the Kaiser did *not* say, will last longer than Bairnsfather's " Old Bill " or Raemaker's cartoons ; and the words " A Scrap of Paper " will be remembered when the song of " Tipperary " and Elgar's " Carillon " are forgotten.

A buzz of gratulation passed down the table at this neat stroke on the part of our hostess, but her husband rather destroyed the effect by saying :

" The last time Paderewski was here, my dear, you told him that music soared above poetry because the emotions stirred by it were ineffable."

To which Margot, nothing dismayed, retorted :

" Ah, but I was speaking under the spell of his playing ! "

It was on this occasion that I, for the first time, crossed swords with her. I have had several little bouts with her since, but she has never shown the least inclination to be more than guardedly polite to me, so my knowledge of her is chiefly founded on observation and the comments of those who have been more to her taste.

That first fencing-match was a pretty good example of her style in debate, so I print it here in full. The subject was " philanthropy," and I gave it as my opinion that charity neither blesseth him that gives nor him that takes.

" Why ? " she called out. And instantly there was a lull in the general conversation. Our thrusts and parries were only accompanied by grunts of approval or groans of disapproval.

" Because," I said, " the giver is secretly ashamed of the recipient's gratitude and the recipient feels ashamed at having to acknowledge an obligation."

" I hope you speak for yourself," said Margot ; " I have never felt ashamed of giving. If anything I have felt elevated by the pleasure of giving."

" You get pleasure out of feeling you are doing a kind action ? "

" Why not ? "

" Then you are easily pleased. But how do you know that you confer pleasure by the action ? "

" Because the recipient tells me so."

" He couldn't very well tell you anything else, could he ? " I queried.

" I should in his place if I didn't feel it ! " affirmed Margot stoutly.

" Does it never strike you," I went off at a tangent, " that the suggestion of inequality in charity-giving may be very humiliating to the object of your charity ? "

" Our religion teaches us the very reverse of that."

" Do you always abide by your religion ? "

" In belief—yes."

"Well, your religion says it is more blessed to *give* than to receive——"

"Exactly. And the comparative 'more' proves that it *is* blessed to receive as well as to give."

Finding myself cornered there, I asked:

"Then you find nothing humiliating in the division between riches and rags?"

"No more than Christ did."

"And you cannot conceive the acute sense of mortification felt by the destitute when the wealthy throw them a bone?"

"You overstate the case."

"Believe me, no! It is an ever-present factor. And I myself feel thoroughly ashamed of my clothes and my cleanliness whenever I give a beggar a shilling."

"So that's why you've stopped doing it?"

This sally of hers was rewarded with a hearty laugh from the listeners.

"Yes," I said, "I live up to my spats nowadays and give half-crowns."

"You are too sensitive," she continued. "One must take the world as one finds it, and it's better to give than not to give."

"If I did take the world as I found it and acted throughout on your advice I'd soon be in Queer Street."

"There is moderation in all things," she replied.

"'Sell all that thou hast and give to the poor,'" I quoted—"not much moderation about that."

" A diplomat can cite scripture for his purpose,"
came the quick retort—and I had to confess to " a
hit, a very palpable hit."

Margot is certainly a hard hitter, and she can
receive blows as well as she can give them. But as
she is utterly impervious to irony, a tilting-match
with her yields small satisfaction to the other
combatant.

§3

Mayfair swarms with people who make a cult of
good living. I mean that they really think of nothing in
the world except their comforts and their luxuries.
With these people even sympathy with the poor is
a form of personal indulgence. It is pleasant to feel
one is leading a " useful " life, or it is delicious to
be occasionally subjected to waves of sentimental
fraternity, or it is ravishing to feel thoroughly
unselfish for, say, half-an-hour a week.

There is no earthly reason why they shouldn't be
like this. I am not passing a moral judgment. I
am simply stating a fact. Most of them can't help
it. The rest wouldn't help it if they could. Altogether, to a dispassionate observer, it is a most
intriguing state of affairs.

The consequence of all this is that the people who
cater best for the indulgence of the many are the
most popular. The hostess who can serve up first-
class oysters out of season (as though the oysters
themselves had risen to the occasion by request) is

" divine." The host who can bring a shoal of sturgeon, swimming in tanks, straight from the Caspian Sea, and present his guests with caviare that was literally in a generative condition an hour or two before it was placed on the table, is " a perfect dear." And anybody, male or female, who can provide these epicures with a new sensation is " simply IT."

Now the Countess of Warwick has done pretty well all these things. She provided Society with a new sensation when she became a Socialist, and Society has shown its gratitude by inventing scandal about her ever since—which, as you may know, is the highest tribute Society has the power to pay. But that is not all. She has also, and always, been an admirable hostess. She knows exactly what people want. She has studied the fads and tastes of every individual who sits at her table. Does the Duke of Rutland like olives ? His Grace shall have a plate of olives by his side at every meal. Does the Marquis of Anglesea feel the cold ? There shall be a hot-water bottle at his feet during dinner. Has Lady Warrender a penchant for parsnips ? Parsnips she shall have both in and out of season.

She even remembers who likes who and sees to it that " incompatibles " are not forced to endure one another. And then there is always the person who " simply must " have a talk with the lion of the occasion, and the lion of the occasion who " flatly refuses " to be introduced to a certain person. All such matters she bears in mind, and it is not too much

to say that nearly all her functions go off without a
hitch.

I once stayed at Easton Lodge, and I do not
remember ever having been so comfortable. The
Countess is, beyond doubt, an ideal hostess. She
thinks of everyone and seems to have an eye on
everything—a sort of mental eye that travels about
the house and grounds and is in every room and
every part of the garden at one and the same time—
an omniscient, omni-present eye.

What's more she invariably seems to be on the top
of her form, so I presume there is neither bottom
not midway condition. At meals she literally irra-
diates—there is no other word to express the brilliance
of her talk, the quickness of her comprehension, and
the lightning-like rapidity with which she will forestall
a want or turn an argument. I think she is the
wittiest woman I have ever met, and certainly the
youngest in spirit.

It is because she is so young in herself that she
likes to surround herself with young people. I
fancy H. G. Wells must be the oldest of her constant
visitors, and he is not exactly senile either in body
or in mind! And though I was only just over
fifty when I was her guest for an all-too-brief week-
end, I felt an " old dodderer " in the midst of that
chubbily youthful house-party.

What particularly struck me about Lady Warwick's
conversational wit was its kindness. The rapier
never pierced ; it touched, and then glanced off. I

cannot do better than extract an example or two from my diary.

" When are you going to write your ' life ' ? " asked a young fellow who had been listening open-mouthed to her rapid characterization of certain politicians.

" When I have ceased to live it," she answered.

" That's a mistake," said a well-known surgeon half-way down the table ; " all the best books have been produced when their authors have been in full possession of their vitality. Why wait till all the zest of living has gone in order to recapture the zest ? "

" Why give to the past what is meant for the present ? " returned Lady Warwick.

" In that case you shouldn't write it at all."

" Oh, but I must have something with which to occupy my old age ! All old people should write their lives."

" Why ? "

" For the sake of the young who would otherwise be sacrificed to entertain them."

" Are the old as selfish as all that ? "

" Oh, dear, no ! They are very unselfish. They are so unselfish that they go to any length to amuse the young. And the young are so unselfish that they go to any length to pretend they are amused."

Everybody was charmed by that. It touched us all—and glanced away harmlessly, forgotten in the merriment of the moment.

Shortly after, Lady Warwick was asked by a Liberal M.P. whether she really believed in the creed of the Socialists—and if so, why? Of course the question was not quite so abrupt as that. It arose naturally out of the conversation, but even so it struck some of us as not altogether in the best taste. Her ladyship was not in the least perturbed, however, and parried the stroke in a manner that has received the sanction of the centuries.

" I will answer that if you will first of all tell me whether you really believe in the creed of the Liberals —and if so, why? "

" Liberalism speaks for itself."

" It certainly does at election-time."

" Well, I do believe in it."

" Excellent ! But why ? "

" Because it means Progress without Revolution."

" Then we are comrades, because Socialism also means Progress without Revolution."

" I don't see that. You want to alter our political and economical system at a blow."

" We certainly want to alter them—but if possible with a caress."

" You'll never do it by kindness, and most of you know it."

" Well, of course it *may* be necessary to force people to be Christians." This with the sweetest imaginable smile.

" I don't believe in force," from the Liberal M.P. ; " you will never bring about any reforms worth having unless you convince people that they are good."

" So we shall, all in good time.   The force I spoke of is the force of conviction."

" But people hate interference by the State."

" So the opponents of Socialism keep saying."

" And the State always bungles whatever it touches."

" So the Liberals and Conservatives are never tired of repeating."

" But isn't it true ? "

" I don't think so.   You are the only representative of the State present in this room and I refuse to believe you could bungle anything."

The M.P. was utterly unprepared for this and he remained gaping for about half-a-minute while the rest of us rocked in our seats.   But the button had never left his antagonist's foil, and he was soon following our example. . . .

I can, by the way, add a note on the subject of the Countess of Warwick's " life " which may be of interest to some future historian.   The morning following the incident I have recounted saw a resumption of the discussion that had terminated with her delightful bit of chaff about youth and age. Again she was asked why she hadn't written her reminiscences.   Whereupon she told us, under pledge of a secrecy which time has now removed, that just before the war she had been at work on them and had called in the assistance of an eminent literary man, whose name I would rather not disclose.

Shortly after the outbreak of war her collaborator had gone to America—more from necessity, I gathered, than from choice—where he had bought or started a paper in which he had fulminated against England and written " revelations " of English social life and so-called " portraits " of English notabilities. Among other things he had regaled the readers of his magazine with stories of the great which he had obtained while working on Lady Warwick's memoirs, and had actually reported confidential conversations that had taken place at her table.

She was of course furious about it all and the affair had so sickened her that she had abandoned the work *sine die*. I learned that her friend and neighbour, H. G. Wells, had been bitten in the same way by the same man, and altogether the whole incident had left rather an unpleasant taste in her mouth.

Yet she spoke of the man himself with an admiration not untinged by affection ; and I couldn't help thinking that if, while speaking, she had seen him walking up the drive, she would have hurried forward and welcomed him with that charm which has captivated princes, peers and plebeians alike. . . .

§4

Max Beerbohm has recently contracted the habit of denying everything he is reported to have said or done, so I am prepared for his complete denial of what follows. It must of course be very annoying for a wit, who is trying his hardest to live up to the proprieties demanded by a dignified marriage and a decorous retirement, to have to live down his past witticisms. I can fully sympathize with his decent determination to break with the past. I can sympathize with it, but I must not regard it. Max belongs to mankind, not to the cloistered solitude of Rapallo.

I count myself as one of his most enthusiastic admirers. I think he has written the best essays in the English language. For me, at any rate, he out-Lambs Lamb. But I refuse on that account to treat him with tenderness. Indeed it is precisely on that account that I am unable to do so. If I did not admire him so much, I would not be so irritated by his sometimes quite painful conventionalities.

Max is a respectable paradoxer and an unexceptionable cartoonist. He always has been—in spite of his occasional and almost accidental deviations from verbal and delineal rectitude. The statement calls for amplification.

There is all the difference in the world between a cartoonist like Will Dyson and a cartoonist like Max. While Max is just touching off a few human peculiarities, Dyson is busy satirizing the whole human species. In the same way there is a fundamental dissimilarity between a paradoxer like Shaw and a paradoxer like Max. While Max is saying funny things to make people laugh, Shaw is saying funny things to make people squirm. The average man is tickled by Max and irritated by Shaw; he is consumed by laughter when he sees a Beerbohm caricature, and consumed by fury when he sees a Dyson caricature. Max is " delightful "; Dyson is " damnable." Max is " a sport "; Shaw is " a horror." That is why I call Max a respectable paradoxer and an unexceptionable cartoonist. No one could take the least exception to him. He doesn't cut deeply enough. He is a jester, not a seer.

But what a jester he has been! Surely the most high-spirited and fascinating leg-puller we've ever had. A humorist who, once upon a time, could pull his own leg as well as anyone else's—to our infinite delight. But Rapallo has been the death of him. He has begun to take himself seriously. Those delicious impertinences that used to be handed round furtively among his friends—he would like to destroy them now. His jokes are becoming heavy—weighted with the years—and even a little inept. He actually suffered a severe stroke of snobbery when, a few years ago, the papers told him that his cartoons of Edward VII were not quite in good taste.

No, there seems to be little doubt that the spirit of Puck has left him. Two or three letters that he has written to the papers of late prove that his elfish light is spent, and those of us who loved the dear departed may well ask " Where are the jests of yester-year ? "

My personal contact with him was brief and

unforgettable. It occurred many years ago in a house at Hampstead. There were perhaps a dozen of us present, and Max treated us to at least one memorable display of his characteristic whimsicality. There were other flashes, I am convinced, but I only find this one in my diary.

Some cats were kicking up a terrific shindy outside, and for a moment the feline question monopolized the conversation. I happened to say that they were useless beasts and ought for that reason to be exterminated. Max promptly took up the cudgels on their behalf:

" Your chief objection to their existence appears to be that they are useless," he argued; " but that is my chief reason *for* their existence. In a sordid, materialistic, utilitarian age, they are our sole artistic dispensation. Without them we would lose our certain and single link with beauty. If they were abolished they would be our missing-links with art. Conceive a catless world! One could never again look a kettle in the face."

While we laughed, he finished his glass of wine, and then proceeded:

" The cat's one claim to our affection and admiration is its utter uselessness. It teaches us the value of contemplation for its own sake. It does nothing. It produces nothing. It has no opinions. Its development is not retarded by hatred or love or any positive emotion. It arrives at no conclusion. It looks upon the world and sees that it is good.

It accepts life. It is the only absolute realist in the world of organic matter.

" By merely being itself it has inspired some men to write exquisite poetry. By exactly the same process it has inspired others to think of suicide or slaughter. To both inspirations it has remained supremely indifferent. In a world of busy bees and still busier beetles (of the human and insect variety) it remains the solitary and flawless example of complete comatosity. The virtue that resides in all forms of static art finds in the feline tribe its ineffable expression. Like art, the cat justifies its existence by being what it is. We must accept it, simply and gratefully, as ' cat for cat's sake.' "

Here someone interjected the statement that cats had their domestic uses.

" Their domestic drawbacks, you mean," corrected Max. " Yes, I regret to say they have. They kill mice. They fight dogs. They catch flies. And sometimes they even condescend to prey on garbage. But, fortunately, these activities do not seriously interfere with the even and futile tenor of their ways. On the whole they remain quiescent and spineless. And who would have them otherwise ? The Egyptians worshipped them because they were so, and for no other reason.

" Descended, as we know them to be, from the gods ; uncontaminated by base toil and untamed by man for his still baser ends ; they grace the home

and symbolize the spirit of invincible independence
and sublime egotism."

He paused. A butler took advantage of the hiatus
to refill his glass. Max looked round the table,
shuddered slightly, and added with considerable
feeling :

"Incidentally I hate the sight of the beasts !"

§5

One could write volumes on the changes in mental
attitude of almost everybody one knew during the
war period. Most people were subject to phases
of frenzy, fits of depression, bursts of patriotism,
moments of humility, gusts of revenge, and even
intervals of Christian charity—mood following mood
with a breathless and bewildering rapidity. Futile
optimism was succeeded by whining pessimism,
glowing hope by frantic despair. Altogether it was
an amazing revelation and proved, I think, once and
for all, that, except for a few choice specimens, man
is uncivilized and uncivilizable. Sooner or later he
will have to be scrapped. Left to himself he will
of course scrap himself in time—in spite of the
prophets and the few choice specimens. It will be
rough luck on these last, but the proportion is not
high enough to make the matter a subject for tears.

I have had the good fortune to meet several choice
specimens ; and assuredly one of the choicest was
Walter H. Page, American Ambassador to the

Court of St. James during the war years. I think he was about the sanest, most level-headed, man I have ever met. Alone among my diplomatic confrères he was not the prey of passions. This is not to say he was without feeling. Very much the reverse. He was intensely sensitive, and I never knew a man who was so susceptible to kindness and injustice, to good and evil. But he never once gave vent to the rancour and malice, the degrading prejudice and partisanship, that were the chief stock-in-trade of so many of us. His admiration of a thing was always balanced by a series of very critical qualifications, and his hatred of a thing never blinded him to certain virtues in the thing he hated.

Very vividly I recall a dinner in Westminster shortly after the sinking of the " Ancona " in the Mediterranean. Page was there and appeared to be willing to discuss everything except the war. But he couldn't evade it for long, and at length the inevitable question of American intervention popped up.

At one moment during the talk that followed my eyes happened to fall on Page, who was several places away from me on the opposite side of the table. He was listening carefully, but saying nothing. What particularly struck me, however, was the fact that his cheeks were taut and the muscles showed through them—this giving the almost unmistakable impression that his teeth were clenched. Clearly the conversation was not to his liking, or at least he couldn't trust himself to join in it. I couldn't doubt for a moment that he was suffering pretty acutely from some form of suppressed emotion, and my heart went out to the man.

When he did speak, a little later, it was in a perfectly collected and almost toneless manner, as of one who was only half-interested in his subject. But I knew better than that, for I had seen him in the throes of an emotion that was very far removed from indifference.

I shouldn't think a single human being in Christendom said less that he would wish to recant, from 1914 to 1918, than Walter H. Page. If he felt a thing strongly, he kept it in check as strongly. I will guarantee, from a fairly extensive personal experience, that he was the sanest-minded and sanest-spoken public man in Great Britain during the period of his Ambassadorship. Sometimes it was quite difficult to get him to commit himself even on a matter that had no political or diplomatic significance.

Though I liked him and admired him more than I could say, I had to admit, whenever tackled on the subject, that I had never met a man with whom it was more difficult to get on close terms of confidence. Perhaps he consciously wore a mask of reserve; perhaps he never felt the need of intimacy; perhaps he was of a retiring nature. I cannot say. All I can say is that I never got to know him properly; and that, although we often chatted together for a few minutes at this levee or that function, we only once got further than the "Nice-weather-for-the-time-of-year" stage of sociability.

Fortunately I kept a minute of that one occasion upon which we came to grips. It took place after a quite informal and therefore enjoyable dinner-party in the early part of 1916. Page had been holding forth on certain ethnological matters and giving us the benefit of his wide reading and close observation.

While he was selecting a "Corona," I asked him why he thought England had touched and passed the zenith of its power. It was in connection with our treatment of the Indian races that he had ventured that opinion.

"You will have mothered and fathered the better part of the universe," he replied; "what more do you want?"

"An answer to my question," I said with a laugh.

"Well, it strikes me in this way," said Page. "There's something wrong with your atmosphere. All of you who stay at home are fossilizing. . . . Now you've asked for this, so you mustn't take offence. . . . Whenever a Briton goes abroad he becomes a different man. Why, look at your colonials! They wouldn't stand for the sleepy, muddling-along, old-fashioned, red-tapey ways in which you do things here. No, it's my firm and certain conviction that long before another century is out England *as* England will be a back number. But she'll have peopled the greatest countries in the world, and the nation that takes her place will call her ' Mother '."

" Do you find us so difficult to get on with, then ? "

" Not difficult. That's not the right word. Easy, too easy, if it comes to that. No, I find you just tiring. . . . But I don't know what it is. I can't be angry with you for long. The best of you is the best in creation. It's unapproachable. But the worst is—well, it's just tiring ! "

" Don't you think there's any hope for us ? Surely if we pulled ourselves together we might yet stay where we are ? Or can't we help ourselves, and it's simply our turn to go under ? "

Page thought for a while. Then he spoke quietly, deliberately, and with a hint of strong feeling in his voice :

" A nation gets old as a person gets old. One hardly notices it until it's there. It has come so stealthily. Then, suddenly, one wakes up to the reality that one's limbs won't function as they used to and one's memory wanders and one's hearing is a little difficult and one's sight a bit hazy. That's what has happened to England. For a time your old age gave you caution—and during that period you very wisely seized the financial control of Christendom —but even your caution is deserting you now, and you cannot renew the freshness of your ancestors. . . .

" If the population and government—especially the government—of Australia or Canada could change places with the population and government—

244

especially the government—of Great Britain, there
would be some hope for you. But as it is, in spite
of your heroic qualities, your endurance, your
chivalry, your unselfishness, you cannot last. Your
brain is going, and you are going at the knees. You
are too old. The centuries bow you to the ground.
Tradition fetters your limbs. The past clogs the
present . . . . But we nations that have the sap of
youth in us are grateful to you for giving us the
strength of your stock. Your greatness will live
on in us. America is England's immortality. . . ."

I don't think any of us were particularly elated
by the prospect he sketched—perhaps it was a little
too true to be pleasant, but Page's sincerity was as
unquestionable as his sympathy. Indeed, there was
a " catch " in his voice as he spoke the last words—
and, no Englishman ever being equal to these
emotional occasions, the matter was pursued no
further.

§6

I met Whistler two or three times in the early
nineties, but as he belonged to a different generation,
and as I was not in those days especially interested
in modern painting, I can't say the meetings meant
very much to me.

Nowadays I realize that he was a truly big man,
one of the greatest figures in the history of his art;
and though I cannot hope to repair my early negligence

I can perhaps throw a little light on certain unfamiliar aspects of his character.

Whatever knowledge I here display was gleaned chiefly from talks with men who knew him well, both friends and enemies ; though luckily I shall be able to round off the picture with the record of an incident in which I took part.

Whistler was a man of moods. He was not all things to all men, but different things to different men. He was instantly and wholly affected by personality. That is to say, a complete stranger was able, without knowing it, to rub him up the wrong way or stroke him down the right way. The gentleness of his response to sympathy and the violence of his response to antipathy were immediate and complete. And indifference was to him just as hostile as open antagonism. He that was not with him was against him.

The interesting thing about Whistler as a human study—and one of these days he will be the subject of a fascinating biography—is that in him all the common traits of humanity were intensified. He had more pride than the proudest man, more humility than the most humble. His quickness to take offence was only equalled by his readiness to forget an injury. His scorn out-blasted the derision of some, his generosity outdid the liberality of others. The sting of his cruelty could only be compared with the balm of his kindness. Within the same hour he could be demigod and devil. . . .

The net result was, I need not say, that people either loathed him or loved him. There was no half-way house. And it is because people have set down such totally contradictory views of him that he seems enigmatical. But the fact is that he was extraordinarily simple. Indeed, one could almost call him a primitive. The complex man does not usually inspire affection or hate, but rather a qualified liking or a qualified disliking. Nor does the complex man react, as Whistler did, so vigorously to such purely external factors as the sound of a voice, the shape of a nose, the expression of a face, the shake of a hand.

Whistler in that sense was a child, a spoilt child, the kind of child that is at one moment up in the skies and at the next moment down in the dumps. His humour could turn into sarcasm at a second's notice, and his best friends could never feel quite sure that he wouldn't be treating them as his worst enemies in a week's time.

It so happens that I can show him in two apparently irreconcilable moods at one and the same time. They are not really irreconcilable, except in the sense that human nature is irreconcilable. But they would be called so by writers who know nothing of human nature—i.e. the vast majority of writers. Those of us who are not mentally fogged by standards and generalizations and rules of conduct know well enough that the only thing one can predict about human nature is that it is unpredictable.

At a time when he was being dunned by half the tradesmen in Chelsea, a young artist who was in great distress begged him for a loan. Though he was slaving away to pay his own creditors and hadn't a penny in his pocket, Whistler journeyed over to the fellow's studio in Notting Hill, painted him a picture, which he was able to sell at once for £100, and then returned home.

Standing at the door of his house in Tite Street and ringing his bell was a local newsagent to whom he owed 7s. 6d. The man touched his hat and begged the great artist to settle this small account, mentioning that he had called for payment on several previous occasions.

"I suppose," said Whistler, annoyed by something in the man's manner, "I suppose you imagine I haven't the money to pay your silly little bill."

"Oh, Mr. Whistler——" began the tradesman with a deprecatory gesture.

"Well, you'd be quite right," Whistler cut in, "because I haven't. Good-morning."

The newsagent began to expostulate, but Whistler was by now on the other side of the door, from which post of vantage he treated the other to a valedictory comment:

"You must have wasted quite seven-and-sixpence-worth of time by coming to see me," said he.

Then he slammed the door; and though the poor tradesman may be forgiven for calling him a brute and a scoundrel, the opinion of the artist he had just helped must also be taken into account.

Another good instance of Whistler's instability of attitude was given me by a friend who died just after he had begun a long biographical article on the artist for some quarterly review.

" Here's a true story that I can't tell in this article because the editor would cut it out," he said. So he gave me the story.

Whistler was very fond of a certain famous actor, who, though married, was separated from his wife and lived with his " leading lady." Naturally the artist saw nothing wrong in this arrangement, and he often visited the couple at their cottage on the Thames.

But one day the actor aired his views to a newspaper representative on the subject of an exhibition of Whistler's pictures that were then the talk of the town. He remarked, among other things, that Whistler, though undoubtedly the leading artist of the day, could not be compared with the great painters of the past—it was too early yet to see where he stood. In the same interview the actor discussed his own arrangements for the future and spoke enthusiastically of his " leading lady," who, he said, went from triumph to triumph.

The cutting was sent to Whistler and several friends were present when he read it.

" Ah ! " he exclaimed, as he threw it into the waste-paper basket, " I see my dear friend —— has again been blowing his own strumpet."

Some other dear friend repeated his little jest—and there were no more pleasant week-ends at that riverside cottage.

As I have said, my personal knowledge of Whistler was confined to a few brief meetings. Either I was too absorbed in other people and other topics to notice much about him, or he was not shining on those occasions. I do not know. The fact remains that nothing worth printing appeared in my diary. Once only do I find extended reference to him. Here it is, word for word :

" After lunch I found myself with Seymour and Whistler in a corner of the room. Seymour had apparently been talking of art, because Whistler was saying, ' My dear fellow, it's no good your talking to me about painting ; I don't even know what qualifications you have to talk of it.' Seymour, who evidently wanted to hear Whistler hold forth, swallowed his pride and answered, ' I have no qualifications at all.' Whistler's eye lit up at once. ' In that case,' said he, ' you will not talk to me, but I will talk to you.' There followed a fairly respectable stream of paradoxes, of which I recollect the following: ' It is only by being unaware of the facts that one creates anything.' And in the course of his disquisition he referred to the Bible as ' a book which, once put down, can never be taken up again.' He talked in a lazy, drawling manner, and I noticed that he glanced at me out of the corner of his eye whenever he made a joke—presumably in the hope that he would catch an answering glint of appreciation.

"After he had let off all his squibs, Whistler turned suddenly to me and asked whether I admired Titian. 'Very much indeed,' I replied, ' though I don't know a great deal about him.' Without pausing an instant he retorted 'Quite so. Quite so. Your ignorance explains your admiration, dear boy' —and before I could think of a serviceable answer he was talking to someone else on the other side of the room."

§7

When a man tells you that he is " a born Bedouin," nothing that he does is likely to surprise you. I was staying with Sir Hugh Lane in Chelsea when Augustus John was busy doing frescoes in his hall and dining-room. The job, by the way, was never completed because the work shocked a certain lady, so John told Lane that he would have to decide between art and the proprieties—and marched out of the house!

It was during my first talk with this refreshing rebel that he described himself in the words I have quoted, and in that way I became more interested in the man than in the artist. And indeed, fine artist though he is, I think John is far more remarkable as a specimen of humanity. Certainly in England, where rebels do anything except rebel. One knows so well the usual type of British " bolshie." His words are so courageous, his actions so pusillanimous.

His epigrams are daring, but his engagements are decorous.

With him actions speak quite as loudly as words. For his own sake it is fortunate that he is not a Socialist. Had he been, his healthily rebellious nature would have kept him incarcerated for the greater part of his life. But being only an Individualist, however fierce and riotous, he has been allowed the fullest possible licence.

" A lot of damned idiots call this an individualistic state of society!" he cried, making Sir Hugh's crockery rattle as he thumped the table. " It's about as individualistic as a flock of sheep. There's no law to keep you together, but by God! you all follow one another through the same gap in the hedge of convention."

" That's all very well," I said, " but where's your freedom going to stop? Do you believe that everyone in the world should do exactly as he or she likes, without let or hindrance ? "

" I do ! " he shouted.

" Then what's to prevent my murdering you ? "

" You can bet your boots I'll prevent it ! "

" You've no safeguard. Suppose I sandbag you from behind ? "

" You have my full permission to try it on."

" Thanks very much, but I should want a King's pardon before I tried."

" But you seem to assume that if people were free they'd want to murder one another," he went on.

" If that were true, half the races in the world would have perished long ago. Murderers are in a minority, and even laws can't stamp them out. I believe that if people were absolutely free they'd be quite harmless socially. They'd only be harmful to themselves, and that wouldn't matter. Restrictions turn people into criminals. Give 'em what they want and the so-called criminal class would soon die out."

I'd often wanted to meet one of these out-and-out free-thinkers and free-livers, and now at last my wish was fulfilled.

John is a stark realist and a stark rebel. He believes in getting everything he can out of life.

A night or two spent out of bed has about as much effect on him as a glass of champagne has on most people—if anything, it brightens him up a bit.

" Yes, I'm fond of work," he said on another occasion ; " that is, I'm fond of the work I'm fond of ; but life was made to *live* ; and work, even the work one likes, comes a long second."

He certainly lives his life fully—perhaps over-fully—and his self-assertive, masterful, care-free, ravenous manner of living it terrifies the men of his generation who were birched into submission before they began to taste the joy of living.

During the war he reduced some of his seniors to such a condition of nervous paralysis that his language became more formidable to them than the unexpected appearance of a German Army Corps on their front. Staff officers trembled at the name of John and quailed at the mention of Augustus. No one knows the number of times he was *nearly* court-martialled. But it is doubtful if even Kitchener would have had the courage to do the thing properly.

At one extra-early morning parade, John, who had had a pretty heavy carousal the previous night and had only been in bed for about two hours, said something to his Colonel that the latter didn't relish.

" If you don't take very great care, I'll have you up for insubordination," warned the Colonel.

" If you don't take very great care, I'll have you up for indecency," retorted John.

" How dare you, sir ! " yelled the Colonel. " What the hell d'you mean ? "

" No decent person ought to be able to pronounce ' insub ' . . . whatever the word was . . . at this time of night," answered John.

It was, I am told, absolutely necessary that John's superior officers should cultivate and propagate a sense of humour.

*   *   *   *   *   *   *

So closes my gallery of personalities. As to the people I have tried to paint, I can honestly say that I have neither belittled nor belauded them ; and though I may have removed some of them from their frames, I have never distorted their features.

THE END

INDEX

255

INDEX

INDEX

257

INDEX